Edited by:
Savonna Gooden-Smith

Book Design by
PGEE Graphic Design
pgee.graphic@gmail.com
(410) 793-7238

Photography & Videography by:
Daniel Mack & Prolific Photos Media
prolificphotos@yahoo.com

Table of Content

ACKNOWLEDGMENT

FOREWORD
Bishop Dr. Stephanie Jennings Stratford

PREFACE
Bishop Joseph A. McCargo Sr.

INTRODUCTION – Defining the term Doyen

The Methodology

–

Acknowledgment

First, I want to thank God through the Lord Jesus Christ for inspiring me to fulfill my lifelong dream of obtaining my doctoral degree and allowing me to write my first book chronicling my pursuit into the leadership. I thank those leaders in business and ministry who have inspired and stimulated my mind and character, pushing me to exhibit the highest attributes and characteristics necessary to lead in my lifetime. To my father in the faith, Bishop Joseph A. McCargo Sr., Senior Pastor & Founder of the City of Hope @ The Energy Centre in Columbia, Maryland and the President and Founder of the International Network of Churches, Ministries & Businesses thank you for allowing me the opportunity to glean from your life and ministry. To my mother in the faith, Pastor Sheryl Menendez, Pastor of Light of the World Family Ministries in Glen Burnie, Maryland, thank you for being an inspiration in my life. Your humanitarianism and community efforts along with your commitment to ministry has pushed me to be the man that I am. Lastly, I thank my wife, Savonna Gooden-Smith, for her love and support throughout my journey. When I look into your eyes, it is the motivation that drives me to greatness and your smile is the approval that satisfies my inner ambitions. You are the medicine that satisfies my soul. Your love invigorates and stimulates me every day. You have believed in my dreams and fostered my aspirations as your own, loving me harder when things became tougher. I love the love we have! I also thank my sons, Dominic Jeriah, Jalen Tekel, and Desten Tyvonne who are my legacy and the reflection of my life's work as a father, husband, leader, and businessman. I treasure being your father and greatest supporter.

FOREWORD

Bishop Tyrone Smith's work on *The Making of a Doyen Leader* is inspirational, reflective, and informative. It presents a biblically supported exposition of doyen models of leadership from the creation of man to the ultimate example of our Lord and Savior Jesus the Christ and beyond. This work provides vital principles that must be employed by those who endeavor to lead in the Kingdom of God. It will also be challenging and thought-provoking to all who claim the Name of Christ.

Bishop Smith raises the expectation for doyen leadership beyond public display and examines leadership as exhibited through obedience, worship, sacrifice, and mentoring in Kingdom leaders. *The Making of a Doyen Leader* sets forth obedience and subsequently self-leadership as the foundation of exemplary leadership. It provides a blueprint for leaders that will transcend their calling and become a legacy for those who will succeed them.

Bishop Tyrone Smith personifies the doyen leader. His presence and practices in the Body of Christ have equipped countless believers and led them to pursue ministry excellence. This body of work will be a guide to those who endeavor to epitomize Kingdom leadership. It will also serve as an indictment against those who carry the title but do not walk worthy of the high calling that is in Christ Jesus.

Bishop Stephanie Stratford, D.Min.
Presiding Bishop, Ekklesia International
www.drstephaniestratford.com

PREFACE

As we study various individuals who have served in the office of various levels of leadership, we see different leadership types and styles, from monarchs to dictators, evolutionists to generals, Hollywood heroes and business icons. What we need within our societies today is real leadership, strong, intelligent, scalable, educated and well versed in domestic and foreign affairs. Having the capacity to surround themselves with influencers and thinkers that do not just fill an open spot but supply strengths beyond themselves. Everything hinges upon leadership whether in the U.S., UK, India, UAE, and even in the undeveloped countries, there is a new type of leadership emerging. They believe that they are called for such a time as this. They are passionate, they are intentional.

In this expository, the writer, Tyrone Smith, explores a new descriptive 'The Doyen Leader'. He has been on the cutting edge of both faith based and marketplace collaboration for many years. Hidden within these pages you will discover his level of brilliance. As you peruse and allow him to strategically take you into this new space, I am sure that your view of leadership will certainly be enlightened. The whole world is looking for change. The future has tapped you on the shoulder to be the change the world is looking for.

Bishop Joseph A. McCargo Sr., President
United Kingdom Network of Churches, Ministries & Businesses
Twenty 1st Synergy's Inc.
www.bishopjam.com

Introduction

During my time of study, I was introduced to the term doyen. The term doyen (doy·en) means the most respected or prominent person in a particular field; a person considered to be knowledgeable or uniquely skilled because of a long experience in some field of endeavor. After an examination of the term and the careful consideration of the leadership, I recognized the necessity to pursue such a place in every area of my life, marriage, business, ministry, and parenting. My desire through this expository is to stimulate the mind of the readers to acquiesce to the methodology of achieving a place of prominence in their lives by pursuing a greater knowledge of God through Systematic Theology and not by the obtaining of a title or position of prominence only. Systematic Theology as stated by Elmer L. Townes in his book "Theology for Today" takes the material furnished by Biblical and Historical Theology, and with this material seeks to build up into an organic and consistent whole all our knowledge of God and the relations between God and the universe, whether this knowledge be originally derived from nature or from the

scriptures. [1]Ray Bakke's book "A Theology as Big as The

City" speaks to us on this wise, "this principle seems clear: the

further one goes into the avant-garde frontier of creative

ministry, the more important it becomes that we be deeply

rooted in the biblical, theological and historical tradition.

This writing will also explore an important observation

of relevance within doyen leadership to avoid self-intoxication

of one's perception of greatness and prominence.

[2]Contemporary Theology analyzes current thinking regarding

Christianity. Inasmuch as Christianity must always be

expressed in contemporary terms, the validity or non-validity

of each person's expression of Christianity must be examined

and verified. Within each [3]theological dispensation, a true

measurement of doyen and relevance is clearly expressed by an

---

[1] *Ray Bakke, A Theology as Big as The City (Downers Grove, IL; Intervarsity Press 1997) p.27*
[2] *Contemporary Theology, Elmer L. Townes Theology for Today Copyright© 2002 by Wadsworth Group, p.35*
[3]*Theological Dispensation (as defined by dictionary.com) is a divinely appointed order or age.*

individual's ambition to follow God, by the leading of the Holy

Spirit, beyond the scrutiny of its generation, nationality, and

ethnicity. If we consider the Apostle Paul to substantiate this

argument, he writes in Philippians 3:14, I press toward the

mark for the prize of the high calling of God in Christ Jesus,

which offers an objective and subjective view of his pursuit in

Christ. Objectively, he knows that God has called him, and he

steadfastly commits his life to the fulfillment of that calling.

However, subjectively it is clear that his desire to fulfill that

calling has a deeper contrition and surrender to the Holy Spirit

which affords him a revelation his counterparts did not have.

To say, "I press" means to move into a position by exerting

force and clearly Paul continually moved into a position that

has earned him prominence within the canonical writings of the

scriptures. In Ephesians chapter 3:1-5 NKJV, he allows us to

see what this "press" has done to him; For this reason I, Paul,

the prisoner of Christ Jesus for you Gentiles— if indeed you

have heard of the [a]dispensation of the grace of God which

was given to me for you, how that by revelation He made

known to me the mystery (as I have briefly written already, by which, when you read, you may understand my knowledge in the mystery of Christ), which in other ages was not made known to the sons of men, as it has now been revealed by the Spirit to His holy apostles and prophets. Throughout this writing, I will carefully exegesis the scriptures to further authenticate the Apostle Paul's life in contrast to other Apostles in his day.

In my daily pursuit to be doyen, I have graduated to the audience of great thinkers, theologians, and authors who challenge this desire with composites that motivate me every day. I will employ many of these great minds throughout this writing to help us in our exhibition of thought and invite the readers to join me in this propinquity of kindred hearts toward the excellency of our faith and leading in God.

Chapter One

The Methodology

In the Beginning - Doyen Obedience

From the very beginning, the [1]Anthropos was God's
greatest creation. The distinction of this fact can easily be seen
in the development of the world; the creation of the heavens
and the earth, the creation of animal life, and the creation of
human life. An expository of Genesis 1 and 2 offers a contrast
between the world's creation and the animal life vs. the
creation of man. Genesis 1:1-25 KJV God demonstrates his
authority in creation and his creative genius by uniquely
speaking everything into existence. A careful observation of
the scriptures allows us to see the continual statements "and
God said" indicating the sovereignty of His power displayed
with his voice. However, in Genesis 1:26 KJV He changed His
approach with the development of man by speaking the
blueprint of his sovereignty and earthly rule and uniquely

---

[1] *Anthropos (as described by The NAS New Testament Greek Lexicon) a
human being, whether male or female*

1

making this man "after his own image and likeness." It is also

noteworthy that this distinction was equally given to both the

male and female creation (v.27), which illustrates an equal

authoritative governing in the earth and over its creation. This

sequestering was followed by God's blessing in v.28 and an

outline of man's governing with God substantiating all His

work and divinity by saying in v.31 "and God saw everything

that He made and behold it was very good." After everything

was created in Genesis 1, Genesis 2 opens with God resting

from His work and during this time of "rest," he changed the

methodology of evolution by forming the man from the dust of

the ground and breathing into his nostrils the breath of life

(Gen. 2-7). These two distinctive characteristics in the

evolution of man's existence proves the difference in God's

view of everything he created vs. the evolving of the

Anthropos. There is no denial of God's power through His

voice however there is a [1]sagacious view of the Anthropos that

---

[1] *Sagacious (defined by Merriam-Webster.com) of keen and farsighted penetration and judgment.*

required "His voice and His hands," offering a clear bias towards man's existence vs. all other creation. This sagacity from God required reciprocity from the man He created which yields the first act of doyen leadership, obedience. Man's first assignment of authority was to dress and keep the garden while maintaining the accountability of eating what was permissible and not permissible to eat from the trees. Doyen obedience starts from the simple comprehension of commands. If we want to be the most respected within our sphere of influence, we cannot reduce the commandment of God to a [1]peccadillo, thinking our behavior will not merit a weighty response from God which inevitably has seasonal and/or generational consequences. As we journey through the early chapters of Genesis, we will explore the consequences of man's reprehensible behavior. After man's early exhibition of authority, God brings to light a deficiency that He needed to know. Man was alone and needed an equal companion to share in this exploration of authority. The uniqueness of this

---

[1] *Peccadillo (defined by Merriam-Webster.com) a slight offense.*

discovery allowed God to demonstrate his compassion toward man and to fulfill His blueprint He spoke in Genesis 1:27. But, there were several things that had to happen for this compassion to be fulfilled without God appearing to be mendacious[1]. Since the earth was already created, everything God spoke into existence was now an established law or principle. Genesis 1:11 has a unique principle. It says, "Let the earth bring forth grass, the herb that yields seed, and the fruit tree that yields fruit according to its kind, whose seed is in itself, on the earth." This principle in the earth meant anything from the earth had within itself the ability to yield after its own kind. Although He spoke to the grass, the herbs, and the fruit trees, mankind was evolved from that same earth and an [2]aberration would change all the principles God had already substantiated. So instead of going back to the earth to create the woman, He placed the man in a comatose state, open the man

---

[1] *Mendacious (defined by Merriam-Webster.com) not honest: likely to tell lies.*

[2] *Aberration (defined by Merriam-Webster.com) an instance of being different from what is normal or usual.*

and retrieved what he needed, and closed the man up and

presented his need to him. Man, being completely coherent and

doyen in his obedience, knew his assignment was to name

everything in the garden and continues to fulfill his purpose by

naming his need, woman (Gen. 2:21-23). This [1]philosophical

theology yields an important view of consistent obedience from

man and reverence to the sovereignty & continuity of God's

will for the Anthropos, which would later define God's

unfailing love after the fall of Adam "the first man" and the

reconciliation of that man through the Second Adam, Jesus

Christ. Although [2]existentialist or neo-orthodoxy thinking

offers a starch contrast of these biblical facts, one thing is

extremely clear, God's continual admiration for the Anthropos

always answered the question of man's mortal liabilities with

divine [3]coalesce between himself and HIS creation. After

Adam's declaration and pronunciation of this woman, he

---

[1] *philosophical theology - Elmer L. Townes Theology for Today Copyright©
2002 by Wadsworth Group, p.15*
[2] *existentialist or neo-orthodoxy – Robert T. Boyd World's Bible Handbook
Copyright© 1983 Harvest House Publishers*
[3] *Coalesce (defined by Merriam-Webster.com) to unite into a whole.*

uttered man's first prophecy stating, "therefore shall a man leave his father & his mother and shall cleave unto his wife: and they shall be one flesh (Gen. 2:24 KJV)." Later, this prophecy would be substantiated by the Apostle Paul in Ephesians 5:28-32. Although the truth of this prophecy is without question, every act of obedience will be met with an equal act of temptation. When the serpent came to beguile the woman, it was the temptation to challenge the truth of God's command to Adam in Gen 2:8-17. There is debate to the responsibility of the woman's act of disobedience sense she was not evolved until Gen 2:22 however a careful observation of the scripture sheds an important light to this indiscretion by the woman in Gen 1:26-28. When God said, "let us make man in our," the use of the term "man" is interpreted as Anthropos (mankind) which is consistent to the blueprint of creating this image in v.27 when he said, "in the image of God created he him; male and female created he them." This statement indicated everything he spoke was equally shared in responsibility because of the divine blueprint. However, the argument continues with the contrast of creation vs. evolution.

The woman's actual embodied presence was absence during

the actual command given to the man in Gen 2:17 but her

subliminal conscience was fully awake and coherent. We gain

this knowledge through her response to the serpent's inquiry,

"did God really say you must not eat the fruit from any of the

trees in the garden (Gen 3:1 NLT)?" If the woman had no

[1]subliminal conscience, how would she be able to offer any

response to a statement you never heard? It is clear in her

response to the serpent; she knew God's prerequisite

concerning the tree of the knowledge of good and evil. What

can also be observed in this dialogue between the two is the

serpent's knowledge of the truth as well. With these facts

outlined in the scriptures, we also discover a pattern of

behavior in the serpent's persistence to cause the Anthropos to

fall. In a deeper view of the conversation between the serpent

and the woman, he revisits the statements and acts that

---

[1] *subliminal conscience (defined by American Psychological Association Dictionary of Psychology) a level of consciousness at which a stimulus may affect behavior even though the person is not explicitly aware of it.*

inevitably cost him his place in heaven. In Revelation 12, the Apostle John shares a vision he saw concerning a woman and a dragon. In this vision he gives the account of a woman giving birth and the dragon standing in front of her as she was about to give birth, to devour her baby as soon as it was born. He speaks of a war in heaven between the Archangel Michael and the dragon. During this war, the dragon and one third of the stars of heaven are thrown to the earth. Why was there a war? Isaiah 14:13 renders the answer; I (satan) will ascend to heaven and set my throne above God's stars. I will preside on the mountain of the gods far away in the north. I will climb to the highest heavens and be like the Most High (Isa 14:13 NLT). Satan's (the dragon) desire was to be equal with God and he convinced one-third of the stars of heaven to believe this idea. It is the same idea he planted in the mind of the woman in Gen 3:4-5, "you won't die!" the serpent replied to the woman. God knows that your eyes will be opened as soon as you eat it, and you will be like God, knowing both good and evil." Satan has deluded the Anthropos throughout his existence, only proving his [1]demagoguery through deception, blurred facilely, and

manipulation. For the Anthropos to maintain his victory over

satan, he must resist the duplicity he presents through

egocentric characteristics to lure mankind away from the will

of The Almighty God.

---

[1] *Demagoguery (as defined by Merriam-Webster.com) a leader who makes use of popular prejudices and false claims and promises to gain power.*

Chapter Two

Cain and Abel - Doyen Sacrifice

After the fall of the Anthropos, God judges them and establishes the Adamic Covenant; hostility between Satan and Eve and her descendants, extreme pain for the woman in childbirth, strife in the marriage, the curse of the ground and the struggle to live from it, and the introduction of death. After the judgment, Adam changes his address for the woman and calls her Eve, the mother of all living. Ironically at the time of statement, Eve had not conceived any children which indicates Adam's second prophetic utterance concerning the woman. The first prophecy was Gen 2:23, therefore shall a man leave his father and his mother and shall cleave unto his wife: and they shall be one flesh and the second was Gen 3:20. Genesis 3:20 prophecy manifests in the opening of Gen 4:1-2, Adam knew his wife and she conceived baring Cain and Abel into the world. Each brother had a distinct grace; Abel was a keeper of the sheep and Cain was a tiller of the ground. These attributes would prove to be pivotal when each brother presenting their offerings before the Lord. When Cain brought his offering (the fruit of the ground) into the presence of the Lord, Abel also brought his offering (the firstling of the flock) as well. The Lord respected Abel's offering while not respecting the offering of Cain, which offers an interesting dichotomy between the brothers and their sacrifices. To appreciate this contrast, let us review the evolution of the Anthropos. Gen 2:7 states, the Lord God formed the man from the dust of the ground and breathed into his nostrils the breath of life and man became a living soul. This evolvement lends to the [1]anthropological argument which is also called the moral or psychological argument because it reasons that the higher parts of human nature could never have come from non-intelligent matter. The formation of man from the ground reveals his carnal or mortal body is flesh derived from the earth. However, his consciousness and intellect came when God breathed into

---

[1] *Elmer L. Townes Theology for Today Copyright© 2002 by Wadsworth Group, p.39*

his nostrils, awakening the Anthropos to earthly awareness, and understanding. With this understanding in mind, Cain's offering from the ground would be viewed as earthly or fleshly which the Lord could only offer deprecation. When we examine Abel's offering as a keeper of the sheep, he brings the firstling of the flock to the Lord. This offering would be a "lamb offering" which symbolically reflects Jesus Christ, which according to Revelation 13:8 says, and all that dwell upon the earth shall worship him, whose names are not written in the Lamb's book of life, the Lamb slain from the foundation of the world. The Lord responded to the sacrifice of Cain by saying, you will be accepted if you do what is right but if you refuse to do what is right, then watch out! Sin is crouching at the door, eager to control you. But you must subdue it and be its master. This [1]egalitarian commentary establishes the truth of God's view of the Anthropos and the bias He has for those who desire to do right versus those who seek to be egocentric. When

---

[1] *Egalitarian (as defined by Merriam-Webster.com) relating to or believing in the principle that all people are equal and deserve equal rights and opportunities.*

the brothers left the presence of the Lord and began to talk

about the encounter they had in His presence, the

uncontrollable sin God spoke of arose in Cain and he killed his

brother Abel. Shortly afterwards, God visits Cain and asked

him, "where is your brother?" The egocentric character of Cain

responds by saying, "I don't know, Am I my brother's

keeper?" This response indicates the unknown understanding

that God is [1]omnipresent, present everywhere at the same time.

God is in all things and God is close to everything that has

existence. This pedagogy is extremely important to the moral

conscience of the Anthropos and is consistent with the early

encounter God had with Adam and Eve after eating from the

tree of the knowledge of good and evil. Upon eating this fruit,

their eyes were open, and they sewed fig leaves to hide from

each other's nakedness. But, when they tried to hide from the

presence of the Lord because of their act of disobedience, He

asked a question in their hidden place, "where are you?" This

---

[1] *Elmer L. Townes Theology for Today Copyright© 2002 by Wadsworth Group, p.119*

statement was not an indictment on God's omnipresence but a moral questioning to the Anthropos' conscience and egregious behavior. Proverbs 15:3 states, the eyes of the Lord are in every place, beholding the evil and the good. Cain's immorality toward his brother was met with a stern response from God. However, there are two extremely important observations that define doyen sacrifice. The first observation happened when the Lord says, He heard the voice of thy brother's blood crying to Him from the ground. This statement suggests the influence blood has with God and the uniqueness of its language that only God can understand. The second observation reveals the power of blood in redemption. Abel's sacrifice (the lamb offering) was not just any lamb but the first lamb indicating a pure sacrifice that was separated from the others and given to God to overlook anything wrong (sin) that God did not approve. Doyen in sacrifice will always offer unto God the best in sacrifices not knowing when that offering will cover your brother who is wrong (in sin) with God. Abel's blood pleads with God concerning his brother's sin and his offering unto God saves his brother's life from the wrath. This truth can be examined by the curse placed upon Cain in exchange for slaying his brother. His sin magnified the intensity of the Adamic Covenant spoken to Adam, "now you are cursed and banished from the ground, which has swallowed your brother's blood. No longer will the ground yield good crops for you, no matter how hard you work! From now on you will be a homeless wanderer on the earth (Gen 4:11-12 NLT)." Cain's [1]ignominy was great and burdened with concern to those that found him wandering in the earth, so God marked him to warn anyone who might try to kill him. This display of doyen sacrifice is also innate in Matthew 22:36-40, "Master, which is the great commandment in the law? Jesus said unto him, thou shalt love the Lord thy God with all thy heart, and with all thy soul, and with all thy mind. This is the first and great commandment. And the second is like unto it, thou shalt love thy neighbor as thyself. On these two commandments hang all the law and the prophets."

---

[1] *Ignominy (as defined by Merriam-Webster.com) public shame or disgrace.*

Chapter Three

Nadab and Abihu (The Doyen Worship) 21st Century Priesthood (Lifestyle)

The honor and dignity of a priest is birthed from an extreme

responsibility and accountability unto God. The contrast

between a protestant priest and a catholic priest is clearly seen

through their lives, though similarities exist, the distinctions are

precise. In Catholicism, the Trinitarian view of God, the birth

of Jesus Christ, the use and following of the scriptures

(Catholics use Douay-Rheims or Knox Version of the Bible

which possess other books not found in the traditional King

James Bible), Salvation that leads to Heaven and Damnation

that leads to Hell (although they believe in [1]Purgatory), and

many other doctrinal beliefs are shared with the Protestant

Church. However, propinquity of its daily practices and

---

[1] *Purgatory (as defined by Encyclopedia Britannica Dr. Carol Zaleski, Professor of Religion, Smith College, Northampton, Massachusetts. "Purgatory", updated 21st Mar. 2021.) the condition, process, or place of purification or temporary punishment in which, according to medieval Christian and Roman Catholic belief, the souls of those who die in a state of grace are made ready for heaven.*

devotions are very different. In Catholicism, the priests practice

their administration of the liturgy in the church, but their

prayers and personal devotions are left to their own discretion.

Whereas, in the Protestant Church the priest study the Bible,

pray, and participate in fellowship or interaction with the

parishioners daily. Though this difference seems small, the

merit of this difference is [1]monolithic with the church's [2]milieu

and expectations are completely at opposites. One group has a

demonstrative approach to [3]Philanthropy and the acts of good

seen by society. While the other group expresses a deep and

consistent life of devotion and dedication to God, publicly and

privately. This observation in the Protestant Church's

leadership raises the standard of the moral and ethical behavior

that is exhibited throughout the world, knowing the canvas of

their lives are always seen and assessed. In [4]Bill Hamon's

---

[1] *Monolithic (as defined by Merriam-Webster.com) huge, massive.*
[2] *Milieu (as defined by Merriam-Webster.com) a person's social environment.*
[3] *Philanthropy (as defined by Merriam-Webster.com) goodwill to fellow members of humanity.*
An active effort to promote human welfare.
[4] *Apostles, prophets, and the Coming Moves of God by Bill Hamon Destiny Image Publishers ©1997 Biblical Principles of Ministry Chapter 3 p.39*

Book "Apostle, Prophets and The Coming Moves of God," he shares his view of a leader's (Apostles in this case) character. He states, their character will be in line with the fruits of the Holy Spirit (Gal. 5:22). Their attitudes, actions, and relationships with others will be according to the attributes of agape love as revealed in 1st Corinthians 13. All of their "10 M's" of Manhood, Ministry, Message, Maturity, Marriage, Methods, Manners, Money Morality, and Motive will be working in their lives according to God's divine order." In lieu of this reference, we glean from the scriptures the [1]predilection of Leviticus Chapter 8-10. Chapter 8 begins with God instructing Moses to bring Aaron and his sons with their sacred garments, the anointing oil, and their offerings for ordination. This sacred consecration was performed by Moses in the presence of the people with a water washing of Aaron and his sons and public dressing in their priestly garments. Afterwards, he anointed the tabernacle and everything in it as well as Aaron

---

[1] *Predilection (as defined by Merriam-Webster.com) a preference or special liking for something; a bias in favor of something.*

and his sons to solidify the holiness of priests and the

tabernacle. Special animal sacrifices were offered and the

blood spread upon the altar, all instructed by God. This

prerequisite was the necessary blueprint for a priest to be set

apart for the working of the tabernacle and the oversight of the

people. However, all these sacred acts were done after the

penitent acts of Leviticus Chapter 1-7. These chapters reveal

the preparation and sacrifice for peace, sin, and guilt of the

people as well as the priests. It is extremely important to note

the number of chapters dedicated to the preparation of the

priest and the people in contrast to the dedication and public

consecration of priest. It is clear after perusing these scriptures

that the preparation of the people and the priest far exceed the

ceremony and public consecration. The [1]perfunctory of the

priest can easily be traced back to the [2]repudiate preparation of

the priesthood and the lack of reverence to the expectation of

---

[1] *Perfunctory (as defined by Merriam-Webster.com) lacking in interest or enthusiasm.*
[2] *Repudiate (as defined by Merriam-Webster.com) to reject as unauthorized or as having no binding force. to refuse to have anything to do with: DISOWN.*

God's commands. If there is no admiration and dedication in the infancy of the priest, the maturation will be stagnated and laced with a reprehensible behavior and their work will be paltry and without merit. Another characteristic to the priesthood that must be observed is the circumventing of God's law to the satisfaction of the Anthropos' will. [1]A law is an expression of the will of the lawgiver. As such, it has five characteristics: (1) those who are subject to the law, (2) an expression of will (the standard of expectation, (3) punishment for deviation, (4) reward for compliance, and (5) it assumes a lawgiver. When there is a sincere capitulation to the divine law of God, the earthly benefits are immeasurable, but non-compliance yields detrimental liabilities. When reading the opening of Leviticus Chapter 10, there is an aberration from God's command of ceremonial worship from Nadab and Abihu that resulted in their death. An exegesis of this scripture not only reveals disobedience to God's law but a deeper broach

---

[1] *Elmer L. Townes Theology for Today Copyright© 2002 by Wadsworth Group, Chapter 3 - Theology Proper Section VI p.129.*

between an older generational subordination to God vs. a younger generational subordination to God. In the same Chapter 3 of Theology Proper Letter D states, the nature of law implies a penalty for the violation of that law. This is the foundation of all government. As a matter of fact, the certainty of the penalty for violating any law depends upon the credibility of the one who enacts the law. Since there is a God, and He rules by His laws, He will penalize those who break His law. In view of Nadab and Abihu's action, there seemed to be [1]circuitous liberty to offer unto God a clear deviation of the expected sacrifice with no cognizant thought of penalty. This paradigm can also be compared subjectively to the 21st century priesthood, employing the objective view of [2]antinomianism. The distinction between antinomian and those (Christians) who view the moral law is its belief and obedience to the law is motivated by an indwelling principle flowing from belief rather

---

[1] *Circuitous (as defined by Merriem-Webster.com) Being or taking a roundabout, lengthy course.*
[2] *Antinomianism (as defined by Merriam-Webster.com) one who holds that under the gospel dispensation of grace the moral law is of no use or obligation because faith alone is necessary to salvation.*

than pressurization derived from any external motives, knowledge, or censorism. Having a strong predilection to God through the sensitivity of the Holy Spirit allows the Anthropos to honor and receive the entirety of the Bible, not segregating its authenticity because of a differentiating of dispensations. At no time in the existence of man, should God be considered irrelevant or unconscious to the moral and ethical governing of his creation. Hebrews 4:13 NLT states, nothing in all creation is hidden from God. Everything is naked and exposed before His eyes, and He is the one to whom we are accountable. This anthropic evolution and its exploration have put great emphasis on knowledge without the consideration of inspiration and guidance by the Holy Spirit. With these facts in mind, we can draw a safe conclusion of Nadab and Abihu's defiance and disobedience as a generational objection that views the law of God and his creed as optional rather than absolute. Even in the canonical history of [1]Eli and his sons. Eli was the high priest of Shiloh and his sons, Hophni and Phinehas behaved nefariously

---

[1] *Eli and his sons - 1 Samuel 2:12–36*

by taking the prime cuts of meat used for sacrifices and by

committing adultery with the women who served at the door of

the sanctuary. This treacherous act by his sons and Eli's lack of

faith in God to subordinate his sons for their wrong ultimately

caused their entire house to be cut off from God. Although

Eli's sons were not priest and did not serve God, the parallel

between these two narratives show one generation that would

follow and honor God and another that chose to disobey and

dishonor Him. This [1]exegetical theology of Leviticus 10 and 1

Samuel 2 offers a clear understanding of doyen in worship and

sacrifice within the priesthood. Somehow in the adaptation and

evolution of the Anthropos, the further we evolve, the more we

become [2]nihilistic. To be doyen in worship and sacrifice, the

[3]inerrancy of the Bible and God must have propinquity in the

conscience of the priest. To live admirable in the sight of God

---

[1] *Elmer L. Townes Theology for Today Copyright© 2002 by Wadsworth Group, Chapter 1 – Prolegomena to Theology Proper Section III p.13*
[2] *Nihilistic (as defined by Merriam-Webster.com) the belief that traditional morals, ideas, beliefs, etc., have no worth or value.*
[3] *Inerrancy (as defined in Theology for Today Copyright© 2002 by Wadsworth Group, Chapter 2 Bibliology Section I, Letter C)*

without a healthy understanding of Bible, will lead to

inconsistency and nebulous characteristics which lends to the

justification of your behavior to satisfy your wrong to yourself

and the public. While musing over Bibliology written in

Theology for Today, there is an interesting commentary shared

about the [1]inerrancy debate from the thoughts of Martin Luther,

A.H. Strong and other conservative scholars. It states, these

scholars have never had to face the problem of those who

denied the inerrancy and inspiration of scripture, although each

generation had to fight its own theological battles, these attacks

were faced and answered by the people of God. The 21st

century priest must strive to display a contrite exhibition of its

worship and dedication, privately and publicly, by avoiding the

early church's refutation and behavioral heresy through

[2]Gnosticism. [3]Even though Gnostics do not have a unified

---

[1] *Elmer L. Townes Theology for Today Copyright© 2002 by Wadsworth Group, Chapter 2 – Bibliology Section VI, Letter C, The Inerrancy Debate*
[2] *Gnosticism (as defined by Merriam-Webster.com) the thought and practice especially of various cults of late pre-Christian and early Christian centuries distinguished by the conviction that matter is evil, and that emancipation comes through gnosis.*
[3] *Roger E. Olson, The Story of Christian Theology: Twenty Centuries of Tradition and Reform (Downers Grove, IL: Inter Varsity Press, 1999) p.68.*

theology, structure, or leadership, they believe that they possess a special and higher spiritual knowledge than that of catholic faith. Rather than the earlier church structure that sought the truth in the collective voices of the apostolic witness, Gnostics had various individual teachers, each with special knowledge to charismatically convey its message to waiting listeners. Their brand of spirituality fostered individual interpretation, spiritual elitism, division, and a fragmentation of the Christian community.

Chapter Four

The Peter and Paul Dichotomy – Doyen in Contrast

Apostle Peter and Apostle Paul were the prominent and most influential voices of the New Testament. Although their conception into the Kingdom of God came at two different dispensations, they were privileged to meet and impact the early church collectively. However, there are some very strong contrasting differences between the two that we will examine with respect to respect or prominence as apostles. To begin the observation of Peter's life, we would certainly have to examine the gospels of Matthew, Mark, Luke, and John. To appreciate the authors and their writing, we observe the target of their writing which defines the emphasis and view each one had of Jesus Christ. Matthew's writing focused on the teachings of Christ, Mark's writing focused on the works of Christ, Luke's writing focused on the parables of Christ, and John's writing focused on the conversations of Christ. This categorizing of the gospels gives any reader a better understanding of how each one sees the life of Christ. Matthew and Mark identify Peter

and his brother Andrew as the first to be called by Jesus. It is

interesting to note that Peter was chosen first, though it did not

mean he would be the lead apostle by his positional selection,

but it does raise an inquiry to his position in lieu of his

influence, relationship, and preeminence in the New

Testament. The other apostles were chosen shortly afterwards.

The chronological order of events differs with each author as

well as the details however Matthew, Mark, and Luke (the

synoptic gospels) share a strong similarity of events. I also

want to identify another interesting observation of their

choosing. The first four apostles to be selected ironically were

brothers, Peter & Andrew, and James & John. However, even

though they were related, there influences differed, and their

prominence varied throughout the New Testament. As we

observe Peter's life through the scriptures, we see an array of

interactions that begin to shape the doyen leadership within

him as well as his foibles. One of those moments happened on

the Sea of Galilee after five thousand people were fed with two fish and five loaves. The story (Matthew 14:22) starts with a

simple and very important command to get into the ship and go

before Jesus to the other side. This command, though

infinitesimal, is the goal of the disciples and anything less

would be considered incomplete or failure. Upon entering the

ship and launching out to sea, the waves became tumultuous

and the winds very contrary. It is important to note that Jesus is

not in the boat with them, He went up into the mountain to

pray. This weather occurrence happens at the [1]fourth watch of

the night which means it is dark with low visibility. During

these moments, Jesus appears on the water but with poor

visibility, the disciples cannot see Him. To understand this

moment of doyen leadership, you must exegesis this story very

carefully and exhibit a clear judicious mind. If it is dark and

you cannot see Him, the waves are tossing the boat, and the

winds are blowing vigorously, how would Jesus be able to

---

[1] *Fourth watch of the night (as defined by Ellicott's Commentary for English Readers, Zondervan Publishing House January 1, 1979, ISBN-10: 0310241200) The Jews, since their conquest by Pompeius, had adopted the Roman division of the night into four watches, and this was accordingly between 3 A.M. and 6 A.M.*

speak so the disciples can hear him? And to offer a greater

view of the scripture, when they finally realized it was Jesus,

Peter challenged Him by asking the question, "if it is you allow

me to walk to you." This statement lends to judicious thinkers,

he was not close to the boat to touch Him, and the sound of the

sea would prevent the disciples from hearing him up close as

well. Peter leaves the boat to walk to Jesus and never gives

thought of defying gravity. However, after walking he looks at

the wind and fear overtook him, and he began to sink. Jesus

walks to Peter, lifts him out of the water and walks back to the

boat. Once they entered the boat, the winds ceased and the

disciples worshipped him, calling him the Son of God.

Unfortunately, they did not know their [1]fidelity was being

tested. In Matthew 8:23, Jesus had already demonstrated his

authority over the winds in a parallel situation, accept this time

he was in the boat with the disciples when the winds became

contrary. After being awaken from His sleep because of the

---

[1] *Fidelity (as defined by Merriam-Webster.com) the quality or state of being faithful.*

winds, he rebuked the contrary winds and said, "peace be still."

Two storms with unique outcomes; Jesus speaks to the storm in

the first story and then appears in the storm in the second story,

to establish doyen leadership. Even with Peter walking on the

water, the command was to go to the other side of the Sea of

Galilee and walking on the water offered an opportunity to

prove genuine respect and prominence amongst his

constituents. Whether theologians and great thinkers observe

this [1]postulation in the scriptures, even as a hypothetical story,

the moral of the story promotes faith in commands and not just

moments of greatness. Walking on the water is great but going

to the other side was the goal and the command the required

obedience, faith, and fearlessness which yields a much better

outcome in view of greatness. Matthew, Mark, and John all

record this story however Peter, who walked on the water did

not. What does this teach us? Anyone can tell your story but

only you can walk it out. When you know the commands to

---

[1] *Postulation (as defined by Merriam-Webster.com) a thing suggested or assumed as true as the basis for reasoning, discussion, or belief.*

achieve your destiny, never settle for a moment of greatness in

the sight of others, who may have never accomplished what

you have done, it was not the goal just a failed moment that

looked good. Peter never referenced this story in the two

epistles he wrote.

The next encounter defined the New Testament church.

Matthew 16:13, Jesus came into the coast of Caesarea Philippi

and asked the disciples, "Who do people say the Son of Man

is?" They all replied by offering different names not realizing

he was searching for someone to identify him as the Christ, the

Son of the living God. In the study of [1]Christology, Jesus used

the term "Son of Man" when discussing his earthly ministry

(Matt. 8:20; 9:6; 11:19; 16:13 Luke 19:10; 22:48), when

foretelling his passion (Matt 12:40; 17:9, 22; 20:18), and in

teaching regarding His return in power and great glory (Matt

13:41; 24:27, 20; 25:31; Luke 18:8; 21:36). Peter was the only

---

[1] *Christology - Elmer L. Townes Theology for Today Copyright© 2002 by Wadsworth Group, Chapter 4 – Christology, Section II Letter D. p.163*

one who identified him properly and, in this [1]logos, rhema was revealed and instituted as the substratum of the church. This exegetical extraction was the first mentioning of the church and Jesus establishes a unique polemic that distinguishes Christianity from all other known religions. He states, "blessed are you, Simon son of Jonah, for this was not revealed to you by flesh and blood, but by my Father in heaven. And I tell you that you are Peter, and on this rock, I will build my church, and the gates of Hades will not overcome it. There are several important points in Jesus' statement; He tells of a divine revelation that only God can release, He makes the distinction that will separate the church from the "gatekeepers of dead thinking," and though "small" in its identity, it would be the foundation the church would be built upon. When studying Christianity, we are the only religion that denotes [2]Trinitarian

---

[1] *Logos - Elmer L. Townes Theology for Today Copyright© 2002 by Wadsworth Group, Chapter 4 – Christology, Section II Letter E. p.163*
[2] *Trinitarian Monotheism - The Stanford Encyclopedia of Philosophy Principal Editor: Edward N. Zalta (Stanford University), The Metaphysics Research Lab Center for the Study of Language and Information Stanford University*
Stanford, CA 94305-4115 ISSN 1095-5054, 2.5 Trinity Monotheism

monotheism in our belief. This belief offers a "three in one" view of God with the third person of trinity existing in man. Peter again establishes a doyen leadership characteristic by identifying Jesus as the Christ and being distinguished by Jesus in the identity of the church. Another prodigious moment in Peter's life was at Mount Tabor (The Mount of Transfiguration). Jesus takes Peter, James, and John up this mountain and while there He is transfigured before them. Again, a judicious thinker would ask, why not take all of disciples up the mountain? Employing hermeneutical thinking, here is a simple explanation. Previously, Peter was able to identify Jesus as the Christ which denotes a "revelation" he possesses. James and John were called "the sons of thunder" during a time in Samaria when Jesus was on His way to Jerusalem. They were met by some villagers who opposed them because they were going to Jerusalem. Since Samarians and Jews did not get along, James and John suggested praying down "fire from heaven" to consume them but Jesus rebuked them for such thoughts and intent. This conviction, though dangerous when it is out of control, is necessary and useful in motives and belief. So inevitably, Jesus takes "revelation" and "conviction" up the mountain to have a life changing encounter. When they arrived, Jesus' face lit up like the sun and afterwards Moses & Elijah appeared. Of course, this all had divine meaning, but Peter had an interesting suggestion. He said, "Lord, it's wonderful for us to be here! If you want, I will make three shelters (tabernacles) as memorials—one for you, one for Moses, and one for Elijah." As admirable as this would seem, the next moment would define the reason why they were there. After Peter spoke this, a bright cloud overshadowed them, and a voice from the cloud said, "This is my dearly loved Son, who brings me great joy. Listen to him." Upon hearing what was clearly the voice of God, the images of Moses and Elijah disappeared and the only person that remained was Jesus the Christ. A careful exegesis of this story would reveal Moses and Elijah symbolically as the law and the prophets. This would confirm what Jesus said in the scripture, do not think that I have come to abolish the Law or the

Prophets; I have not come to abolish them but to fulfill them

(Matthew 5:17). What do we draw as a conclusion for Peter in

this moment verses the characteristic of a doyen leader? Even

though he was not correct in his moment of revelation, he

knows how good it is to have been in this place with Jesus.

When they came down the mountain, Jesus would command

them not to share what happened which would later prove to be

an extremely important [1]exegetical theology at the Passover

supper. [2]In Theology for Today, it references this moment in

Jesus's life. It says, at the ascension of Christ, Jesus was both

glorified and transfigured. He was glorified: "wherefore God

also hath highly exalted him and given him a name which is

above every name" (Phil 2:9). Where the previous glory of

Christ in Heaven was dependent upon His Person, this added

dimension of glory is based upon his completed work. He was

transfigured, in that when John saw Christ on the isle of

---

[1] *Exegetical Theology - Elmer L. Townes Theology for Today Copyright©
2002 by Wadsworth Group, Chapter 1 – Prolegomena to Theology Proper
Section III p.13*
[2] *Christology - Elmer L. Townes Theology for Today Copyright© 2002 by
Wadsworth Group, Chapter 4 – Ascension Section XIII p.249*

Patmos, His face shone, His feet were shining, etc. (Rev. 1:13-18).

Another doyen moment in Peter's life happened at Capernaum. The collectors of the Temple tax inquired about Jesus paying taxes. As with many good followers of their leaders, you immediately defend them without thinking because you love and respect them. However, when Peter went into the house, Jesus asked Peter, "do kings tax their own people or the people they have conquered?" This pedagogy would again substantiate an important point concerning Peter's revelation. It seems as if Peter spoke impulsively and not revelational of the Christ he identified. Peter responded, "they tax the people they have conquered." Jesus replied, "well, then, the citizens are free!" However, the next statement would offer a clearer understanding of this story. Jesus told Peter, we do not want to offend them, so go down to the lake and go fishing. The first fish you catch, open its mouth and you will find a large silver coin. Take that coin and pay the tax for both of us. Why would Jesus be concerned about offending the tax collectors? Doyen in leadership understands subordination and

responsibility. A revelation from God will never override your

accountability to governmental law. If you cannot subordinate

yourself to the "world's laws" how will you obey the laws of

the spirit? Since we are a part of the Kingdom of Heaven, we

are governed by a different ruler who grants you freedom in

relationship. However, in relationship He does not force you to

give, like taxes, He expects you to give because of relationship;

a relationship he paid for with His son Jesus the Christ. The

other pivotal point of reference is where he told Peter to get the

money. When he met Peter, he told him "I'll make you fisher

of men." This symbolism of fish can clearly be identified as the

church or the kingdom. Jesus feeds five thousand with two fish

and five loaves, two typologies that represent the church or

kingdom (The Old & New Testaments) and five loaves of

bread (five is the biblical number of grace and bread

symbolizes the Lamb) denoting the [1]age (dispensation) of grace

---

[1] *Dispensation of Grace - The Seven Dispensations of Grace: Dispensation 4, The Perfection Grace by Karis Maple; Covenant Books, ISBN-10: 1643005030*

through the Lamb of God, which after partaking of this meal,

twelve baskets (governmental law and order) were left,

indicating the Apostolic Age of the church. After reviewing

what Jesus told Peter exegetically, go to the church or kingdom

and obtain the money needed to pay the world so we do not

offend them. This is the doyen way we should function as

leaders.

While eating the Passover supper, Jesus is very troubled

and has a moment of transparency when he says, "I tell you the

truth, one of you will betray me! (John 13:21)" What seems to

be an innocent moment within his mortality is actually a

defining moment of truth for mankind. All twelve apostles are

in this room but more importantly Peter, James, and John; the

fiery sons of thunder and the one who has the revelation of

Jesus, who will later cut off the ear of a centurion who will

attempt to take Jesus into custody. Either of these men have the

capability of stopping Judas from betraying Jesus, which would

alter the pending crucifixion necessary for the redemption of

mankind. Peter, the spokesperson of the group at times, wanted to know who it was however, instead of asking Jesus himself, he leans over to John to ask Jesus the question. Peter was always venerated to Jesus in the past and spoke freely without reservation, why would he be [1]furtive now? It would appear to be a qualitative moment to exhibit the previous doyen characteristics he had displayed before, stepping to the forefront, and leading the questioning. However, asking John would reveal something Jesus had been trying to show Peter all along. In the previous stories, Peter's revelatory insight left him uncertain, unaware, and misguided to the actions and meaning of Jesus' motives. Peter thinks the transfiguration of Jesus on the mountain was the opportunity to build three tabernacles only to see the images of Moses and Elijah disappear and God says, "hear my son whom I well pleased," Peter is demonstrative when confronted about Jesus paying taxes only to be instructed on the benefits of the kingdom versus a monarchy where a king has overthrown the people and

---

[1] *Furtive (as defined by Merriam-Webster.com) done in a quiet and secretive way to avoid being noticed.*

force them to pay taxes. In the Kingdom of God, our freedom affords us the liberty to give without force, which redefined his answer to the tax collectors because he lacked a clear understanding. He walks on the water but inevitably sinks and was saved by Jesus and ushered back to the boat. All these moments, though great in some way, lacked an important characteristic greater than revelation, relationship. When Jesus was transformed in the presence of his disciples, Peter said "it was good for us to be here," but didn't realize how precious the moment was when Jesus commanded them, "don't tell anyone what you have seen," because you cannot tell what must be revealed through relationship. When Peter walked on the water, it demonstrated trust and faith in Jesus even when he could not see Him. A genuine relationship can remain focused in a moment of turmoil, showing a simple but important point of trust, especially if I have given you evidence to believe. The story of the Passover supper is the ultimate depiction of relationship. John was the youngest of the disciples and would always lay his head upon Jesus openly indicating a willingness to trust and be relational even when he did not have the right answers or do the right things. When Peter leaned over to John to ask the question of betrayal, revelation was asking relationship for an answer divine insight could not produce. However, John exhibiting superlative character and maturity with his relationship did not share what Jesus had revealed to him which inevitably secured the secret and the pending crucifixion of Christ. As much as the betrayal of Jesus is worth defending, a deeper understanding of His life, which he spent many days sharing and teaching the disciples, was needed to exemplify the [1]apotheosis of his relationship with Christ.

The chronological order of events leading to the crucifixion differs than the writing in the canon. To understand the events clearly, you would read Matthew 26:1-20, John 13:2-30, Matthew 26:21-29, John 14:1-31, Matthew 26:30, John 15, 16, 17, and Matthew 26:31-75. As Jesus grew closer to the crucifixion, Peter seemed to exhibit flaws within his

---

[1] *Apotheosis (as defined by Merriam-Webster.com) the perfect form or example of something.*

doyen character. After the Passover supper, Jesus shares with the disciples the offense that would cause a scattering of those who follow him, however Peter starchily said he would never be offended because of his relationship with Him. Peter's words seemed contrite, but Jesus would reveal to him a startling truth (that he did not say to any other disciple), before the cock crows in the morning, you will deny me three times. However, Peter vehemently said he would never deny Him. This interesting truth offers a point of reference that everyone must take into consideration. Denial happens when you are uncertain about a matter or if within your comprehensive understanding, there is not enough facts to declare truth. Betrayal however yields a different circumstance of thought. To betray someone, is to have full understanding and knowledge while becoming disloyal and faithless. Although Judas would indeed betray Jesus, he only addressed Peter's denial. This address signified revelation can become distorted if truth has not been totally substantiated. No matter how doyen you maybe, you must always pursue truth as the substratum of your ambition to lead. A person who betrays you has already settled in their heart a perfidy towards the knowledge they have learned about you and nothing you do can change it. Judas represents a people who have learned the truth of Christ and absolutely turn away to the satisfaction of their own carnality and immorality. [1]Though the Bible tells us of sinful acts, it is not a popular book where sinful acts take place. Even though there is adultery and immorality in the Bible, the Bible is not found in places where these acts take place. Even though the bible tells of men getting drunk, the Bible is not found in places of drunkards. The Bible is unique in its call to repentance, in its convicting power to unsettle those who sin, and in its power to convert and transform those who accept its message.

Although there is much to glean in our previous observations, there is more to consider. Peter's love for Jesus could easily be measured by his willingness to follow him

---

[1] *Convicting, Convincing, Converting Power of the Message - Elmer L. Townes Theology for Today Copyright© 2002 by Wadsworth Group, Chapter 2 – Bibliology Section V, Section D p.51*

without questions however, Jesus needed Peter to understand the measurement of that love toward him. His inquiry of this understanding was referenced by two animals, a sheep, and a lamb. The dichotomy of these animals represent maturity and/or age. A sheep can be an adult female, called an ewe, and a healthy male is called a ram, but if the male sheep is a castrated male, it is called a wether. Jesus wanted Peter to know, the only way he could [1]promulgate his love for Him to the world, would be how he loved the people, young or old. No matter how the church proliferates, your love must be consistent and precise. Peter (or the church's revelation) must never allow numbers and novicey to dictate your administration, influence, and relevance in any dispensation or risk losing your voice of influence to the people.

Another test to the doyen leadership of Peter happened in the garden of Gethsemane. Jesus again takes Peter, James, and John (the revelation and the conviction) with Him to pray.

---

[1] *Promulgate (as defined by Merriam-Webter.com) to make (an idea, belief, etc.) known to many people by open declaration.*

He tells them wait a distance away while He goes off to pray. This is another critical moment in the life of Christ because the weight of his destiny is truly upon Him, and He must consult God for assurance. The note worthiness of this story is the reason you bring these three men along while you pray about your destiny. He goes off to pray and when He returns, he found all three men sleep but addressed Peter and asked him, "why couldn't you watch with me for one hour?" Two observations must be considered in this statement, although they were all asleep there is a responsibility upon Peter (revelation) that differs from James and John (conviction) and secondly, Jesus says to him "watch and pray that you do not enter into temptation because the flesh is weak, but your spirit is willing." This is very odd and strange. Jesus brought them to pray but he comes back to find them asleep, addresses Peter only, and says you need to pray so you do not become tempted. What is Jesus telling us? Peter, who represents doyen leadership and the revelation of Christ, must be sensitive in his life to pray because in your leading and insight if you are not careful, you can be leading and revelatory but susceptible to temptations because of the weakness of your flesh. Our revelation of Christ must become practical and irrefutable in our living. If we "fall asleep" in our walk with God, we will become profligate in our faith and domicile to carnality and worldliness. In the [1]Pragmatic Test of experience E. Y. Mullins stated, "I have, for me at least, irrefutable evidence of the objective existence of the Person so moving me. When to this personal experience I add that of tens of thousands of living Christians, and an unbroken line of them back to Christ, and when I find in the New Testament a manifold record of like experiences, together with a clear account of the origin and because of them all, my certainty becomes absolute." Our experiences in Christ build an impenetrable wall of faith and truth.

---

[1] *Pragmatic Test of Experience - Elmer L. Townes Theology for Today Copyright© 2002 by Wadsworth Group, Chapter 2 – Bibliology Section V, Section J p.57*

[1]Once Jesus is taken into custody and brought before Caiaphas and the Sanhedrin Counsel, Peter is by himself. He is confronted by a woman who said he was with Jesus and as spoken by Jesus, he denies him. Another woman came to him and claimed he saw Peter with Jesus of Nazareth and again Peter denies knowing Him. A third time, a group of people came and declared, "surely you were with Jesus because your language sounds just like him," but Peter became [2]petulant and profane to discredit the notion of his association with Jesus. Once these things happened, Peter remembered the prophecy Jesus spoke and became plaintive. It is sorrowful to discover your insight in God cannot keep you from the immorality that lurks within you when it is untamed and uncontrolled by your relationship in Christ. Peter seemingly slipped from the place of his revelation of Christ to an unwarranted disciple whose doyen tendencies have completely diminished. However, upon

---

[1] *Denial of Christ Matthew 26:69-75, Luke 22:55-62, and John 18:15-18, 25-27*
[2] *Petulant (as defined by Merriam-Webster.com) insolent or rude in speech or behavior.*

47

Jesus's resurrection from the dead, Mary Magdalene, and Mary the mother of James, came to the sepulcher to anoint the body of Jesus only to discover that Jesus was not there and the stone that blocked the tomb was rolled away. An angel told them Jesus had arisen and to tell the disciples and Peter that He has gone to Galilee. Now this opens an inquiry to all that Peter did. The angel was very precise to tell these women about the resurrection of Jesus and to inform the disciples and Peter. Why was there an isolation of Peter in his command? It is clear in theology; angels are messengers from God and can only do what they are sent to do. The angel was there to tell them He was resurrected and to inform them to tell the disciples as well as Peter, which is most noteworthy that your revelation may fall short, but His love and kindness never will. God wanted Peter to know that you may fall short, and your insight may not always be there but His love for us will never stop and His Godliness toward us will always be there. Peter would have never known that his revelation, though keen and precise, would take him on a journey of doyen leadership that left him vulnerable and desolate, lost, and despondent, lonely, and lost but in the site of God still venerable and soon to be the preeminent voice on the day of Pentecost. Doyen is not an arrival; it is a journey of learning that grows in you by the availability of learning by the Holy Spirit.

After these series of events take place in Peter's life, a new voice was being formed. His early name was Saul but through the regeneration of his heart his name was changed, and he became Apostle Paul. His acquisition into the discipleship was different from the others. The original 12 apostles we all picked by Jesus Christ, but Apostle Paul has an encounter with Christ that inevitably changed his entire life and theology of God. In the introduction to the [1]Doctrine of God in Theology for Today, it states, there are many reasons to study God, but perhaps we should start with the command, "Be still and know that I am God." There is no greater reason to study God than the fact that God invites us to know Him. This

---

[1] *Elmer L. Townes Theology for Today Copyright© 2002 by Wadsworth Group, Chapter 3 – The Doctrine of God Section I, p.95*

invitation found Paul on the Damascus Road persecuting the early believers, which he himself later confirmed in Galatians 1:13–14. This [1]Christophany changed his view of God and the believers he persecuted which inevitably led him to Ananias, who by a revelation from God, led him to meet Paul (Saul at the time) on Straight Street where he prayed and laid hands upon him to restore his sight (which he lost in the encounter he had with Jesus Christ by the illumination of light). It is interesting to note that Paul's vision was taken in the encounter with Christ. In a hermeneutical view of this encounter, the first thing that had to change was his view of God and Christ. Jesus takes it away and by a supernatural miracle by Ananias, his sight is restored and upon opening his eyes, he is filled with the Holy Spirit. Observe very carefully the dichotomy of the early apostles and Apostle Paul. Act 2 depicts an encounter with the Holy Spirit that yields "new tongues" but Apostle Paul's encounter with the Holy Spirit gives him "new vision." Is this a

---

[1] *Christophany - Elmer L. Townes Theology for Today Copyright© 2002 by Wadsworth Group, Chapter 3 – The Doctrine of Christ Section III, p.173*

mistake in administration by the Holy Spirit? Not at all, but a better understanding of [1]Pneumatology, which would satisfy Paul's commentary later in 1 Corinthians 12. The Apostle Paul's early entry into doyen leadership clearly differs from Apostle Peter, which is evident in Paul's life because right after being baptized, Paul begins preaching Christ in the synagogues by Act 9:20. Paul's exoneration from his previous life to the glorious acceptance of Jesus Christ merited a different response than his predecessors. It took Peter several years to begin preaching but Paul began preaching in several days. A clear-cut distinction of doyen contrast. Although converted, Paul previous antipathy toward Christians made him greatly feared in Jerusalem. Barnabas, a Levite from Cyprus, brought him to the apostles and shared his story of conversion and regeneration. However, the Jews would not receive him and

---

[1] *Pneumatology - Elmer L. Townes Theology for Today Copyright© 2002 by Wadsworth Group, Chapter 5 – The Pneumatology, p.261*

sought to kill him. [1]Conversion is the term most misunderstood term in religion. Often regeneration and conversion are used interchangeably. This confusion takes places in our contemporary media when we say, "born again" and "converted" to become Christian. This is most unfortunate but can easily be resolved in understanding the biblical doctrine of conversion and regeneration. Conversion is the human side of that experience and regeneration is the divine side. Although you could clearly see through the life of Paul, a great change had happened to him but in society there is an interesting aphorism that says, "a leopard never changes his spots," which defines the Jews' view of Paul. After his encounter with Christ, he was never belied in his presentation, he was truly changed but difficult to receive because of his previous life before the conversion and regeneration of his heart. Sometimes doyen leadership comes with constructive castigation, which can hinder your intentions and demonstration of such excellence

---

[1] *Soteriology - Elmer L. Townes Theology for Today Copyright© 2002 by Wadsworth Group, Chapter 9 – Conversion Section VII, p.447*

and prominence. This aggreges behavior of the Jews followed Paul for a good while during his early years of preaching but he continued preaching always knowing his life was in jeopardy.

Paul's life and tenure in the Kingdom of God obviously yielded a different revelation than the other apostles. He referenced this revealed knowledge in Ephesians 3 stating, "you know God gave me the special responsibility of extending his grace to you Gentiles. As I briefly wrote earlier, God himself revealed his mysterious plan to me. As you read what I have written, you will understand my insight into this plan regarding Christ. God did not reveal it to previous generations, but now by his Spirit he has revealed it to his holy apostles and prophets." His statements point to a contrast in dispensations. The "special responsibility" he speaks of affords him a grace to preach the gospel to the gentile believers, that other generations did not have. Ironically, [1]dispensationalist believe that the

---

[1] *Soteriology - Elmer L. Townes Theology for Today Copyright© 2002 by Wadsworth Group, Chapter 9 – Salvation in The Old Testament Section III, p.422-423*

Anthropos is saved by grace through faith in every dispensation. Even so, one of the most oft-repeated charges against dispensationalists is that they teach more than one way of salvation. If any man is saved in any dispensation other than those of Promise and Grace, he is saved by works and not by faith. The methodology of salvation, no matter what is believed to obtain and maintain it, differed between Peter and Paul. This difference can be attributed to "The Apostle of the Lamb" versus "The Apostle of the Church" observation. One man and those with him see the people one way, while another man and his views see the people another way. Peter was with Jesus as he preached the beatitudes; blessed are the poor in spirit, for theirs is the kingdom of heaven, blessed are those who mourn, for they shall be comforted, blessed are the meek, for they shall inherit the earth, blessed are those who hunger and thirst for righteousness, for they shall be filled, blessed are the merciful, for they shall obtain mercy, blessed are pure in heart, for they shall see God, blessed are the peacemakers, for they shall be called children of God, blessed are they which are persecuted for righteousness sake, for theirs is the kingdom of heaven. However, Paul by the inspiration of Christ, writes the fruit of the spirit in Galatians 5:22-26, but the fruit of the Spirit is love, joy, peace, longsuffering, kindness, goodness, faithfulness, gentleness, and self-control, against such there is no law. Those who are Christ's have crucified the flesh with its passions and desires. If we live in the Spirit, let us also walk in the Spirit. Let us not become conceited, provoking one another, envying one another. A different time, a different language, but the same subject and message. Paul told the Romans, "For as many as are led by the Spirit of God, these are sons of God (Romans 8:14). [1]A characteristic of a Christian's life should be his willingness to follow the leading of the Holy Spirit. He is a Person, He can lead, guide, and direct our lives. He is God and has supernatural abilities to help us overcome our temptations successfully by serving the Lord. The allegory of Paul's writing was quite precise to the leading of the Holy Spirit. This

---

[1] *Pneumatology - Elmer L. Townes Theology for Today Copyright© 2002 by Wadsworth Group, Chapter 5 – The Deity of the Holy Spirit Section II, p.274*

doyen leadership exhibited by Paul has been argued and sometimes controversial in the modern age of explaining pneumatology. In [1]section III, "The Procession of the Holy Spirit", this dialectical pedagogy arises from the words of Jesus when he stated, "But when the Comforter is come, whom I will send unto you from the Father, even the Spirit of truth, which proceeded from the Father (John 15:26). The question is how can the Second Person of Deity give directions to the Third Person of Deity and remain equal at the same time? It was not until A.D. 381 that the Council of Constantinople first issued the decree that recognized the Holy Spirit, "who proceeded from the Father." There was a subsequent discussion among early theologians concerning the relation of the Holy Spirit and the Second Person of the Trinity. At the third ecclesiastical assembly at Toledo in A.D. 589, the Latin term "filoque," meaning "and the Son" was added to the statement from at Constantinople. These didactical views of the Holy Spirit have

---

[1] *Pneumatology - Elmer L. Townes Theology for Today Copyright© 2002 by Wadsworth Group, Chapter 5 – The Procession of the Holy Spirit Section III, p.274*

been argued for many years but in its biblical observation, the revealed knowledge Paul has, set him apart from the others, affording him the privilege of writing 13 epistles, while Peter only wrote 2 epistles. Was there a difference between Paul and Peter? Was Peter dilettante in his approach to the gospel and the well-being of the early saints? Was Paul's scholastic academia the reason for his divine insight that gave him such revelation? To these questions, the obvious answer would be no, however Paul's availability to the Holy Spirit and conversion gave him a [1]hegemony amongst those who shared in responsibility of the churches' progression, evolution, and adaptation. All throughout Paul's writing to the churches and those "sons" in ministry he wrote to, provided a divine inspiration of the Holy Spirit and doyen leadership.

[2]The third division of the New Testament opens with thirteen of Paul's letters. The gospel accounts give us the facts

---

[1] *Hegemony (as defined by Merriam-Webter.com) influence or authority over others.*
[2] *Robert T. Boyd World's Bible Handbook Copyright© 1983 Harvest House Publishers Books of the New Testament Division III, The Epistles p.497*

about Christ's earthly life; Paul gives us the meaning of it.
Nine of his letters are called Church Epistles which he wrote to
seven churches. Three are called Pastoral Epistles which he
wrote to pastors (Timothy and Titus) and one to a dear friend,
Philemon. Five of the thirteen epistles are called Prison
Epistles because they were written while he was imprisoned in
Rome. The Church Epistles are divided into three groups. Each
group gives us doctrine, reproof, and correction, which speak
to the logic of the canon rather than the chronologic of the
events. The first group starts with Romans, which is doctrinal,
giving us the mystery of Christ on the cross-outlining
justification and sanctification. Corinthians is for reproof,
detailing the failure as to practical sanctification. Galatians is
correction and the denial of justification by faith. The second
group starts with Ephesians, which is doctrinal, giving us the
mystery of Christ's church. Philippians is reproof, although
there is praise and joy, there is a failure to complete unification
of its members. Colossians is correction, outlining the denial of
the supremacy of God. The third group is completely I and II

Thessalonians, it is doctrinal, speaking to the mystery of Christ coming, reproof to live in holiness and correction to be knowledgeable concerning those who are asleep and apostate. In all these epistles, Paul's language is so different than his comrades, but the subject never wavered. In Romans, there are 60 references from fourteen Old Testament books of which Paul places great emphasis on "the just shall live by faith (Habakkuk 2:4). This becomes the drive to truth in Rome and in the future, becomes the revelation to enable Martin Luther to bring reform into the open. Paul's epistle to I Corinthians, was a church founded during his first visit to the city which lasted 18 months. It was predominately filled with Gentile believers with some Jews, most of them poor, with a few exceptions. Under the Romans, Corinth was a wealthy seaport city, given to luxury, immorality, and heathenistic behavior. During his tenure in Ephesus, he heard reports of immorality amongst the saints in Corinth, which sparked Paul to write a very stern letter, demanding the withdrawal from [1]licentious individuals. However, even though he wrote this letter urging them to stop this behavior, the conditions in Corinth did not change. To this point we must consider a few things; although you exhibit very high doyen characteristics, it does not prevent low demonstrations of character by your followers and all followers do not symbolize its leadership. Corinthians exhibited division, carnality, immorality, litigation, marriage and separation, the misappropriation of the Lord's Supper, and the denial of the resurrection. And with all these heathenistic acts, Paul continued to love them and outlined that love in I Corinthians 13. Again, a different language from his brothers but clearly truthful to the gospel of Christ. This usage of words and theological observation can be found throughout his epistles. His commentary on spiritual children and fathering (I Corinthians 4:14-17), the nine gifts of the spirit and the propinquity within the body of Christ (I Corinthians 12), his

---

[1] *Licentious (as defined by Merriam-Webster.com) lacking legal or moral restraints.*

revelation about The Eucharist (The Lord's Supper), his "Declaration of Independence" in the epistle of Galatians, outlining the liberty from the law through the principle of salvation, the explanation and definition of the fivefold ministry (Ephesians 4:11-16), his ambition and pursuit of the "higher calling" in Christ (Philippians 3), his disposition and satisfaction of encouragement and support he received while in the Roman prison (Philippians 4), the doctrinal errors of Judaism and mysticism (Colossians 2) and his insightful revelation of the pending apocalypse and immorality (I and II Thessalonians) all produce [1]Neologism. The subjects are clearly tied to the birth, life, death, resurrection, and second advent of Christ, however his terminology of words and phrases introduced a new view and etymology of the scriptures.

---

[1] *Neologism (as defined by Merriam-Webster.com) a new word, usage, or expression.*

Chapter Five

Conclusion

Doyen characteristics have been exhibited throughout

the history of the bible. From the evolving of the Anthropos to

the calling of the apostles, this distinction was always

preeminent. God's blueprint in the evolution of Adam begins

the branding by forming him with His hands and breathing into

his nostrils. God's hands and breath in and upon mankind gave

them unique attributes and set them apart from every other

thing he created. This uniqueness was given an accountability

of obedience necessary to maintain solemnity with his creator.

At no point can doyen truly be exemplified without obedience

to a higher calling, power, or presence. The engine that drives

doyen obedience is connected to something or someone's

influence pushing you to be more than philanthropic to the

satisfaction of others but to be demonstrative in your reverence

and dignity to that call or caller (God). Even with mortal

liabilities always available in your life, the [1]parochial view of Christ should inevitably provoke you to recalibrate your errors and push you to be greater than the initial fall.

Cain and Abel are a moral lesson of sacrifice and the necessity to offer God the very best you have. It is clear in the story; God has a partiality to those who come with the best sacrifice versus those who bring sacrifices they feel suitable for God. Mankind's postulation of this fact is nothing more than a paltry denial of God's prerequisites to adhere to his commands vs. the misguided understanding of [2]antinomian. The "God knows my heart" paradigm is the inexcusable attempt to do whatever you think is right in your own eye, in exchange for offering God whatever is left to the moral consciousness of His will. But an even greater view of this story suggests, your best in the site of God will not only please Him but could save someone's life of judgment or severe penalty from God. To be

---

[1] *Parochial (as defined by Merriam-Webster.com) relating to a church parish.*
[2] *Antinomian (as defined by Merriam-Webster.com) one who holds that under the gospel dispensation of grace, the moral law is of no use or obligation because faith alone is necessary to salvation.*

doyen without provocation relies heavily upon a deeper conviction and dedication to God and maintaining a strong predilection toward what is right.

Nadab and Abihu opens the dichotomy of generational reverence for God through the lives of the priesthood. In an age where social acceptance reigns supreme over godliness and righteousness in the site of God, we see a differentiation of views between an older generation versus a younger generation. Although they were the sons of the high priests, their [1]perfunctory to worship God showed a lack of respect to His instructions and expectations. The doyen leadership point in this story outlines the penalty for doing it "your way" instead of God's way and even in other the other examples illustrated, the same outcome was warranted. Doyen accountability merits generational blessing and favor but it does not come automatically. Every generation must

---

[1] *Perfunctory (as defined by Merriam-Webster.com) (of an action or gesture) carried out with a minimum of effort or reflection.*

circumcise their fleshly motives to yield the spiritual desires that please God.

Peter and Paul offer many views of doyen leadership with contrasts and similarities. As we peruse Peter's life through the scriptures, we see the divine influence of God upon his life early, which seemed to make him the primary spokesperson amongst the disciples. His revelation of Christ immediately separated him from the others and became the landmark to the distinction of those who would inevitably accept Christ & walk in the kingdom. One of the measurements of doyen presence is the influence necessary to direct and redirect those who will follow your leading. This pious characteristic is traceable through the spiritual behavior of this leader. Walking upon the water demonstrated courage, faith, and diligence to go where no one else is going and not waiting for another to move. Extremely pivotal to the doyen character of a leader. You must have a genuine commitment to succeed without the [1]trepidation of failure because failure is not a destination but a brief stop on the road to your destiny. Failure can only be what you allow it to be. It is either the springboard to your next or the hinderance to your success. In everyone's pursuit to doyen, the proverbial conquest will always be tied to overcoming adversity, remaining focused, and reaching higher than those around you. At Mount Tabor, Peter's life began to take an unusual turn which lends to the principle of focus. He recognized it was good for him to be there but in the moment of privilege, he misinterpreted the presence of Elijah and Moses with Jesus to suggest the establishing of three tabernacles, indicating a reverence for each one independently. This happens very often with dispensationalist and individuals who deny the logos of the scripture to satisfy an independent secular humanism view of scripture, inappropriately following a soulish exegesis of the canon.

---

[1] *Trepidation (as defined by Merriam-Webster.com) a feeling of fear or agitation about something that may happen.*

Paul's doyen experiences shed a different light on respect and prominence. From the beginning, Paul was immediately thrusted into a display of leadership that differed from those who came before him. His insight, handling, and conviction all seem to differ from Peter. His early interaction with the disciples of John, his conversion of Lydia from the city of Thyatira, his establishing of Thessalonica and Corinth, his teaching and preaching in Rome, his revelation of The Eucharist, teachers & fathers in Corinthians, and so many other illustrations all demonstrate degrees of doyen leadership. Having an insight that others do not see and having the courage to speak it, speaking in a relevant language that others have not heard, establishing an order that others have not seen, and being hated for a life that you no longer live but cannot deny. These characteristics along with others, are the standards by which all leaders must pursue to achieve a place of doyen.

Chapter Six

The Doyen Mentor

The Moses Model (Christophany)

In this section, we will illustrate the doyen model of mentoring. The first illustration will be Moses, a unique individual whose beginning would seemingly disqualify him from such a regarded place of prominence. You are born in Egypt during the time when Israelites had become a threat to Egyptians because of their large population. Pharaoh ordered all newborn male Hebrew children be cast into the river to drown. Your mother hides you for three months and soon afterwards, when she could no longer hide you, she put him in a waterproof basket upon a river and was discovered by the Pharoah's daughter. You are ordered to be murdered but you end up with the daughter of the one who wants you murdered. You grow up in the system of your oppressor but are aware of your roots and later when an Egyptian was brutally beating a Hebrew slave, you murder him. You flee for your life, becoming a shepherd for Jethro, and later marry his daughter Zipporah. Soon after, his doyen experience began. He comes to a bush that was burning however, it was not consumed or did not burn up and as he drew closer to it. An angel appeared to him, and God called out to him. This [1]Christophany established his relationship with God at a different accountability and expectation. When God calls out to Moses to come close, He stops him and says remove your shoes because the ground is holy. There are many ways to position yourself in reverence to the presence of God; kneeling, bowing, laying prostrate, and lifting your hands are all various ways to exhibit reverence unto God. Very few times do you see an act of reverence unto God in the scriptures by removing your shoes. However, God was not just asking for reverence, He was telling him to take off "where you came from" so I can direct where you are going. This was extremely important because he murdered an Egyptian and fled from Pharoah and the Egyptians but, would

---

[1] *Christophany (as defined by Elmer L. Townes Theology for Today Copyright© 2002 by Wadsworth Group) Christ's appearance in angelic form before the incarnation.*

soon be returning as a representative of God. Moses'

trepidation was preeminent, but this interaction was a

redirection and divine doyen calling. Four hundred years of

bondage and cries was being answered by God through a man

born from them and raised by their oppressors. This was indeed

the establishment of a man to be highly respected for

generations to come. Although God chose Moses for such a

task, he seemed to lack [1]temerity for the assignment due to a

"slow" or stammering tongue as well as his denial that the

people would believe in him. God answered these deficiencies

by showing Moses what was in his hand and upon his life and

by allowing him to choose Aaron his brother as an assistant to

speak. Having a lack of courage or the display of weakness is

never a problem with God, He will always show you the merit

of doyen in your life. After a series of events, Moses would

inevitably lead the nation of Israel out of Egypt into the

wilderness for what should have been forty days that became

---

[1] *Temerity (as defined by Merriam-Webster.com) excessive confidence or boldness, audacity.*

40 years. During their time of testing, they became hungry, and God provided manna from heaven and water from a rock (Exodus Chapters 16-17). In Exodus 17, God instructed Moses to strike the rock to obtain water, but later in Numbers 20, Moses was instructed to speak to the rock and in frustration disobeyed God by striking the rock again. This moment of [1]sacrosanctity was a display of Christ as the Redeemer of mankind in the Old Testament and reference by Paul in the New Testament. I Corinthians 10:1-5 says, "I don't want you to forget, dear brothers and sisters, about our ancestors in the wilderness long ago. All of them were guided by a cloud that moved ahead of them, and all of them walked through the sea on dry ground. In the cloud and in the sea, all of them were baptized as followers of Moses. All of them ate the same spiritual food and all of them drank the same spiritual water. For they drank from the spiritual rock that traveled with them, and that rock was Christ. Yet God was not pleased with most

---

[1] *Sacrosanctity (as defined by Merriam-Webster.com) The quality of being holy or sacred.*

of them, and their bodies were scattered in the wilderness. In

Book of Isaiah and Psalms, Christ is spoken of as our Rock and

Cornerstone killed (struck) for our sake, and He will bring

forth the living water, which is biblical [1]Soteriology. Jesus

Christ died once for all mankind with no further sacrifice

needed for sins. Numbers 20 was the second time Moses

struck the rock, which breaks the eschatological prophecy of

the scriptures and brings the anger of God upon him. This

anger would result in a harsh rebuke of Moses which

prohibited him from entering the Promise Land of Canaan.

Earlier we illustrated one of the characteristics of doyen in

obedience. Again, we see the detriment of disobeying God by

missing divine promise. I also want to point out another

noxious behavior that weakens doyen in your life, allowing

others to frustrate you out of God's will for your life.

Throughout the wilderness experience, Moses was confronted

by a nagging, angry, contentious, disobedient people that

---

[1] *Soteriology - Elmer L. Townes Theology for Today Copyright© 2002 by*
Wadsworth Group Chapter 9 Soteriology, Section I Introduction.

pushed Moses to negate this doyen character God wanted him to have. In pursuit of prominence and excellence, we must never lose site of the one (God) who has called us with such a great calling (Ephesians 4:1). After this experience at Horeb, God would require Moses to climb Mount Sinai and spend forty days there to obtain the Torah (10 Commandments). This was such a monumental moment in the history of the Jews because a people that escaped the Egyptian monarchy of Pharaoh, wandering through the wilderness, would tangibly possess evidence that God existed and the validation of its leader in a type of [1]theocracy. This would begin an interesting [2]theophany that would last forty years, starting from Exodus 19 through Deuteronomy 34, a glorious manifestation and development of doyen in Moses' life. God tells Moses about a plan to speak to him in a thick cloud, allowing the people to "listen in" to ensure their belief in Moses and the prophecy.

---

[1] *Theocracy (as defined by Merriam-Webster.com) a form of government in which a country is ruled by religious leaders.*
[2] *Theophany (as defined by Merriam-Webster.com) visible manifestation of a deity.*

After Moses' preparation of the people, the cloud-covered mountain had a loud thunder and a great display of lightning, and the people could hear the voice of God. The people pleaded with Moses to excuse them from the presence of God because of great fear and made a covenant to obey whatever Moses relays to them from God. Moses agreed and assured them what he and God had in mind all along. Moses reenters the presence of God on the mountaintop while the people stayed their distance (Exodus 20:18), and afterward the birth of the law began. As this story continues, God's sanctioning of Moses was clear as the leader and his prominence as a prophet was undoubted. During that time on the mountain, Moses, Aaron, Nadab, Abihu, and the seventy elders were present with God and shared a covenant meal in His presence (Exodus 24:9-11). This Nadab and Abihu are the same two priests that we reference earlier, which offers a greater light to their judgement and lack of doyen accountability to the priesthood. In verse 12 & 13 another distinction of doyen is made. The Lord said to Moses, "Come up to me and stay there, and I will give you the tablets of stone that I have inscribed the instructions and commands so you can teach the people." However, Moses brought his assistant Joshua with him and climbed up the mountain. This admission of Joshua introduces a new candidate of doyen leadership while his predecessor is still present. It is obvious in the reading of the canon that Joshua was being reared to be the successor and not Aaron his brother. From chapter 25 through 31, we see the erecting of the tabernacle, the sanctification of the priests and preparation of the garments. But in chapter 32, while Moses was still in the mountain, the people convinced Aaron to make another god to worship because Moses had been away too long, and the people could not wait any longer. They took gold earrings from the wives and daughters, brought them to Aaron and he fashioned it together and made a golden calf for the people to worship. Aaron made a proclamation, and many offerings were brought while the people ate and drank. When God saw the behavior of the people, a startling statement is made by God to Moses in Exodus 32:7, "Moses go down the mountain! Your people whom you brought from the land of Egypt have corrupted themselves. How quickly they have turned away from the way I commanded them to live! They have melted down gold and made a calf, and they have bowed down and sacrificed to it. They are saying, "These are your gods, O Israel, who brought you out of the land of Egypt." God declared to Moses, it was his people, and he brought them out of Egypt. Even though the people vowed unto God and swore they would obey Him and Moses, their oblivious behavior provided an opportunity to absolutely defy God. Moses sought God to have mercy on the people for their reprehensible act of sin, remembering Abraham, Isaac, and Israel and all the servants that made a covenant with God (Exodus 32:13). Moses' doyen leadership had a profound affect upon God, who repented of the evil he thought to render upon Israel. When Moses came down the mountain to see what the people had perpetuated, Joshua met him to let him know about the noise from the camp (Exodus 32:17). This permission of Joshua to meet Moses at that place on the mountain only further proved a new leader was being formed and he was separating himself from people who [1]obfuscated the command of God, to satisfy their own immorality and carnality. When Moses arrived at the camp, saw the dancing and worshipping of the calf, he became extremely angry and burnt the calf in fire, grounded it into powder, put it into water and made the people drink it. Ironically, the anger he pleaded with God not to have against the people, insighted Moses and made him act out in anger. This [2]malfeasance from Moses in lieu of the people's evil behavior, was another wrongful display of doyen that paralleled his previous action of smiting the rock in Numbers 20. Allowing the people to push you to an anger that prevents you from fulfilling God's plan for your life. Moses would later instruct all that were not on the Lord's side to be murdered and on that day about three thousand men died. This is an interesting dichotomy to Acts 2:41, that after the preaching and

---

[1] *Obfuscated (As defined by Merriam-Webster.com) to be evasive, unclear, or confusing.*
[2] *Malfeasance (as defined by Merriam-Webster.com) wrongdoing or misconduct especially by a public official.*

receiving of Peter's message, they were baptized, and three thousand souls came to Christ. When Moses at Mount Sinai, after the ordeal with calf, the Israelites did not wear anymore jewelry or fine clothes. Moses set up the Tent of Meeting outside the camp so the people could make their requests, and whenever he went to the tent, the people would stand outside their tents and watched him enter. It is interesting to note, when Moses was in the tent, God would speak to him as a friend, and when they were done, Moses would return to the camp, but Joshua would remain in the tent. The current leader would talk to God and leave while the successor would remain in the presence of God. It was becoming clearer as the scriptures read, one leader was fading, and another was forming. One day shortly after the visit at the Tent of Meeting, Moses inquired about the promise land and who would go with him. God reassured him that He would be with him, and everything would be fine however in this dialogue and inquiry Moses asked to see His glory. God told him, he would allow His goodness to pass by, proclaiming His name as he passes by, but he could not see His face and live. He tells him I will be gracious to whomever I want, and I will have compassion on whomever I want and placed him on a Rock next to Him, placing His hand over him and allowing His back parts to be seen but not His face. This rock would symbolize the rock Jesus Christ spoke of in Matthew 16:18, "and upon this rock I will build my church; and the gates of hell shall not prevail against it." This rock (revelation) would be the foundation of the church and no access from hell would triumph over it. God places Moses upon a rock (revelation) to allow His back parts to go by Him but, what is the "back parts" of a spirit? God was not a man with a front or back, so what was He implying here? This conversation started with Moses asking about his future destination in Canaan and who would be going with him. While he is asking about this future, he asks to see the glory of God. God places him on a rock (revelation) to allow what is behind Him to be seen. What is behind God is man's future. God's face represents what He sees, which is the ultimate future of all through His eyes and understanding. To see what

God sees, is to peer into the divine and timeless space where only He has the understanding and wisdom to comprehend. However, His back parts represent His past, which He passes on to mankind as his future. God wanted Moses to see this glorious presence, which was the future of Israel, so he could share it with the people but after witnessing such a presence, when he came down from Mount Sinai and talked with Aaron and the children of Israel, Moses put a veil over his face to hide the glory (Exodus 34:29-33). This exegetical [1]Christophany, is confirmed in 2 Corinthians 3:7-18, "But if the ministry of death, written and engraved on stones, was glorious, so that the children of Israel could not look steadily at the face of Moses because of the glory of his countenance, which glory was passing away, how will the ministry of the Spirit not be more glorious? For if the ministry of condemnation had glory, the ministry of righteousness exceeds much more in glory. For even what was made glorious had no glory in this respect,

---

[1] *Christophany (as defined by Elmer L. Townes Theology for Today Copyright© 2002 by Wadsworth Group) Christ's appearance in angelic form before the incarnation.*

because of the glory that excels. For if what is passing away was glorious, what remains is much more glorious. Therefore, since we have such hope, we use great boldness of speech unlike Moses, who put a veil over his face so that the children of Israel could not look steadily at the end of what was passing away. But their minds were blinded. For until this day the same veil remains in the uplifted reading of the Old Testament, because the veil is taken away in Christ. But even to this day, when Moses is read, a veil lies on their heart. Nevertheless, when one turns to the Lord, the veil is taken away. Now the Lord is the Spirit; and where the Spirit of the Lord is, there is liberty. But we all, with unveiled faces, beholding as in a mirror the glory of the Lord, are being transformed into the same image from glory to glory, just as by the Spirit of the Lord.

Moses' life is a replica of his brother Peter, extremely doyen and insightful to the revelation of God. However, losing focus and not remaining humble caused them to miss God. The only consolation in the view of these two stories is Peter's redemption and opportunity to continue where Moses would die and miss the Promise Land he was called to walk into. Whether it is the Old Testament or The New Testament, the responsibility of doyen remains consistent, you must be obedient, your relationship will always be greater than your revelation, grace is always available when your doyen character is off, great privilege is awarded with such doyen capabilities and attributes, and your life will have a profound affect upon those you lead and cover.

Chapter Seven

The Elijah Model

[1]Elijah, whose name means "Yahweh is my God" is also spelled Elias or Elia in the Bible, a prophet who saved the religion of God from being corrupted by Baal worship. He suddenly appears during King Ahab's reign to proclaim a drought in punishment of worshipping Baal, which Jezebel was promoting in Israel at God's expense. This unusual introduction to Elijah's life immediately intrigues the mind on doyen leadership, not everyone will know about his past or history and neither does it matter to the substantiating relevance of your influence and prominence. Elijah would later meet four hundred and fifty false prophets and four hundred prophets of [2]Asherah, to determine which God was the true

---

[1] *1 Kings 17 KJV Elijah the Tishbite, from Tishbe in Gilead*
[2] *Asherah - Britannica, The Editors of Encyclopedia. "Asherah". Encyclopedia Britannica, 16 Feb. 2018. ancient West Semitic goddess, consort of the supreme god. Her principal epithet was probably "She Who Walks on the Sea." She was occasionally called Elath (Elat), "the Goddess," and may have also been called Qudshu, "Holiness."*

God at Mount Carmel. Two altars were built to see which God would answer by fire and the God of Elijah came and received the sacrifice from the altar. They would slay the priests and prophets of Baal at Elijah's command and Jezebel was furious. Elijah would flee from the wrath of Jezebel and ended up at Mount Sinai. While there, he experiences great sorrow and depression, praying that he would die because he thought he was alone in his fight against Baal. While he was asleep, God sends an angel to minister to him and feed him. Elijah displays [1]equanimity while warring against the false prophets but when he believed he was standing alone, hearing of Jezebel's threats to kill him, he loses hope and desires to die like his ancestors. What happened to Elijah's faith and confidence in God? Surely if He were with him to war against the false prophets, wouldn't He be with Elijah to war against Jezebel? What is more interesting is God's response to the depression, He does not accuse Elijah of having little faith or confidence in Him, He

---

[1] *Equanimity (as defined by Merriam-Webster.com) mental calmness, composure, and evenness of temper, especially in a difficult situation.*

merely sends an angel to feed and encourage him. No indictments of faith or lack of trust and no "remember when stories," only a loving God to a servant in a vulnerable state of morality. Sometimes, doyen leaders have a moment of lapse, when their prominence and greatness is not as good as it should be. This does not demote or degrade the value of doyen but allows a loving God to demonstrate His compassion to His creation. Elijah would travel to Mount Sinai and spend forty days and nights there. While he was there, God told him to stand before me on the mountain outside of the cave where he slept. As he stood there, the Lord passed by him and a windstorm hit the mountain, but God was not in the wind. Shortly afterwards an earthquake violently shook the mountain, but God was not in the earthquake and after the earthquake there was fire, but God was not in the fire. After the fire, there was a still voice like a whisper that spoke to Elijah and asked him, what are you doing here? Like the Moses' experience on Mount Sinai, they were both standing near or in a rock (a cave in Elijah's situation), God passes by but, in the Moses experience He reveals Himself, so He could see His back parts, in the Elijah illustration He allows 3 different things to happen, only to reveal that He was not in any of them but spoke gently in a whisper afterwards. The epitome of this story displays events and situations we determine God is speaking, only to discover that when God wants to speak or reveal Himself, He does not need earthly events or natural disasters to do it. We must be still and know He is God, and He can speak directly to you (Psalm 46:10). He tells Elijah to go back the same way you came, and travel to Damascus. Once he arrived, he anointed Hazael to be king of Aram, he anointed Jehu, grandson of Nimshi, to be king of Israel, and anointed Elisha, son of Shaphat to replace him as God's prophet. This act of doyen is often missed in the current generation because of the lack preparation and resisting to anoint the next leader before you die. This almost never happens. It is the will of God to elicit the next generation of leadership, to ensure succession and continued growth of the people. However, many times the next leader must fight for the position or hope that a divine

[1]empirical happens, yielding the opportunity of leadership. Another true measurement of doyen leadership is knowing when to appoint the next leader without jealousy, envying, or competitive gestures to prove the qualifications to lead. If God has instructed you to anoint them, the excellence of your leadership will be measured in your obedience, not your resistance. When Elijah anointed Elisha, he placed a mantel upon him, and walked away. Elisha was so moved by what happened, he left his oxen standing there, ran after Elijah, and said to him, "I'm going to kiss my father and mother good-bye, and then I will go with you." However, Elijah told him no and instructed him to go back doing what he was doing but think about what had happened. Seems odd that God would tell you to anoint your successor but resist them from following you. But in a careful exegesis of this event, demonstrates two distinct characteristics of doyen leadership; the first is the willingness to obey God without question (which we illustrated

[1] *Empirical (as defined by Merriam-Webster.com) relying on experience or observation alone often without due regard for system and theory.*

earlier) but the second is extraordinarily important, how to discern the intent of your leader. Was Elijah trying to turn Elisha away or use this initial moment of introduction to define his "followship" and determine the strength of his desire to follow him? In 1 Kings 19:21, Elisha returned to his oxen and slaughtered them. He used the wood from the plow to build a fire to roast their flesh. He passed around the meat to the townspeople, and they all ate. Then he went with Elijah as his assistant. Initially he told Elijah he would go and kiss his parents' goodbye and follow him, but Elijah resisted him. Elisha was not [1]acerbic about his actions, but when he went back to serve the people of the town, he could follow and become Elijah's assistant. What a lesson of true doyen leadership. God told me to anoint you, but I need to know your motive to follow me, to become what God has anointed you for. Doyen leaders must never anoint possibility but actuality. Anointing what we think it could be rather than anointing what

---

[1] *Acerbic – (as defined by Merriam-Webster.com) sharply or bitingly critical, sarcastic, or ironic in temper, mood, or tone.*

we know it is, could be the difference between a new leaders' precipice or the inevitable ascension to become doyen. Every anointing must be tested to determine motive, intention, and obedience. From 1 Kings Chapter 19 until 2 Kings Chapter 2, the only thing we know about the Elijah/Elisha relationship is he is there as an assistant. There is no mentioning of his name, no illustrations of mentoring, no stories told of their lives together, and no ministry to speak of. The next time Elisha is spoken of is 2 Kings 2 during a time at Bethel. The company of prophets told him Elijah would be taken away from him on that day, which he responded, "I know but be quiet about it." They leave and go to Jericho and the prophets there told him the same thing and again he replied, "I know but be quiet about it." They leave and go to the Jordan River, where Elijah takes his mantle and strikes the Jordan River and it separated, allowing the two men to cross on dry land. Once they were on the other side, Elijah asked Elisha "what can I do for you before I am taken away?" Elisha replied, "I would like a double portion of your spirit and to become your successor." Again, we have no illustrations of leadership, no stories of their lives together, and

no ministry to give us any information but, in this request of

[1]apotheosis, he reveals the uniqueness of doyen in Elijah's life.

In all the time he spent with Elijah, nothing is mentioned but a

lot is learned, respected, and revered so greatly, Elisha asked

for two portions of his spirit because it influenced him so

powerfully. This request could almost be viewed sacrileges,

asking for the spirit of a man who has received his spirit and

character from God. Which yields the thought, why not ask

God to give you a spirit greater than Elijah? The answer is very

simple, what he saw in Elijah was God operating in a man.

That man was tangible and relative to him, giving him a

blueprint and model, that he could acquiesce to and achieve.

This relationship gave him the perfect illustration of a prophet

and man of God with the moral ethics necessary to please God

and fulfill his assignment. It does not devalue God but

magnifies the doyen in Elijah's life. How well did you live

---

[1] *Apotheosis (as defined by Merriam-Webster.com) the highest point in the development of something, culmination, or climax.*

your life as a leader, when they ask for a double portion of your spirit to fulfill what they will be inheriting from you to serve in the earth? It is the greatest compliment any leader can receive from those who will follow him. The magnitude of doyen displayed without reading in the scriptures is priceless. How many leaders do we know possess spirits worth asking a double portion of? What influences your life that you do not write about, post in social media, or brag about, but absolutely know you want it to lead in your dispensation? Elisha says nothing throughout his time of serving but when asked he wanted 2 times the spirit of his mentor. John Maxwell made this statement about leadership, "leaders must be close enough to relate to others, but far enough ahead to motivate them."

Chapter Eight

The David Model

This individual is one of the most popular characters spoken from the scriptures. So many areas of David's life are preached in the church age and his doyen leadership is a model standard. However, his beginning would suggest greatness was not in his future. He was the youngest son of Jesse and served in the courts of Saul. He was quite the fighter against the Philistines which provoked jealousy in Saul and sought to kill him. He fled for his life and went to southern Judah and Philistia where he established great sagacity to become the leader of Israel. [1]Saul became the king of Israel at thirty years old, a reign that lasted forty-two years, and over that time Saul's humility faded and God had rejected him in his later years because his accomplishments, which created an arrogance within himself. Samuel the prophet was instructed to visit Bethlehem and anoint one of Jesse's sons to be the next king. [2]Instead of

---

[1] *1 Samuel 13 KJV*
[2] *1 Samuel 16 KJV*

picking the oldest and biggest son, he anointed and chose the smaller, younger son, David. The canon is unclear whether Samuel explained to them what this meant. Maybe the family understood his actions (although they would not have a reason to believe he would be the next king without knowing God's plan and the dissatisfaction with Saul) or maybe they thought he was anointed as a prophet, since Samuel himself was a prophet. Whatever the possibilities are in this observation, one thing is very clear, 1 Samuel 16:6-7 defined the proper choosing of any doyen leader. God said, "don't judge by his appearance or height, for I have rejected him. I do not see things the way you see them. People judge by outward appearance, but I look at the heart." This statement should be the hallmark to select any leader in any capacity if the ambition is pure and organic. He spent years on the desert frontier in Judah and became the leader and organizer of a group of outcasts, who gained favor with the local population by protecting them from other criminals and restoring the possessions that were taken. Those actions inevitably ensured him an invitation to become king and the true successor of Saul. Once he became king, he establishes a city in Jerusalem to unite all the tribes. Under his leadership the Philistines were conquered, the entire nation of Israel is unified but more than anything, he served and loved God. Under Saul, the worship of God deteriorates because he disobeyed God's direction through [1]Samuel. The ark of the covenant had been lost for many generations and never returned to its place in the [2]Tabernacle. It was so bad during the reign of Saul, he sought guidance from the witch of [3]Endor the medium. After he destroys the Amalekites and the death of Saul, David is anointed King of Judah. Thereafter, [4]Baanah and Recab found Saul's son Ishbosheth sleeping and murdered him, brought his head back to David as a prize for Saul trying to kill him. But inevitably David would have them killed for such an act. In everything David, he wanted to exemplify doyen leadership especially

---

[1] *1 Samuel 13:13; 15:11KJV*
[2] *1 Samuel 4-6 KJV*
[3] *1 Samuel 28 KJV*
[4] *2 Samuel 4 KJV*

knowing God had been with David throughout his life and ascension to be king. When the time came to retrieve the ark of the covenant, an interesting deleterious happened while bringing it back to Jerusalem. After acquiring the ark from Kiriath-jearim, they made a new cart to place the ark upon for travel. Uzzah and Ahio were guiding the cart as the people sang and played music unto God, celebrating the acquisition of "God's promises," when suddenly the oxen stumbled and the ark was falling to ground, Uzzah reached to save it from falling and God struck him dead. David was angry at God and decided not to bring the ark of the covenant back to Jerusalem but took it to the house of Obed-edom from Gath. The biblical symbolism of the threshing floor is a place of purification and humiliation. Did the oxen stumble or was God symbolizing his dissatisfaction with David's humility and purity in handling his promises? Was there a crack in the doyen fabric that God wanted to reveal in the sight of the people he served? The portent moment would begin a series of events that would later define numerous acts of pride and the lack of humility. It is also important to note that David taking the ark to Obed-edom was not a coincidence. Obed-edom was not the only person from Gath that David knew, Goliath was also from Gath. Did he take it there for that reason to have the same judgement that happened to Uzzah to come upon Obed-edom? There was no mentioning of Obed-edom up to this point, so why did he choose him? God seemingly had [1]Obed-edom at the right place to receive the ark of the covenant which identifies a unique break in generational judgement and the regeneration of one man's heart vs. an entire nation's turpitude against God. Gath was ruled by the Philistines, who were the mortal enemies of the Israelites. Goliath and David battled and inevitably David was victorious but during that battle, David said, "who is this uncircumcised Philistine, that he should defy the armies of the living God?" This declaration identified a starch hatred for the Philistines and his desire to destroy Goliath. However, Obed-edom clearly broke away from the immortality of his people to

---

[1] *1 Chronicles 13-16 and 26 KJV*

pursue a hermetic relationship with God and His people. He lived a life well pleasing to God and well respected by David which brings a contrast to the indiscretion of David's handling of ark. He initially handled it wrong but put it in the right hands until he understood how to move it. Obed-Edom was not just anyone, he was a Levite, a priest in the site of God. [1]Levites and the family of the priesthood were the only ones to carry the ark. Obed-Edom kept the ark of the covenant for 3 months and during that time God blessed him and all his household. So, his right standing with God and moral character earned him blessings from God and his household which broke the curse of judgement from the land of his origin. Once David recognized his wrong, he immediately sought to make it right. Doyen leadership is not being perfect but always seeking to exhibit the moral and ethical behavior necessary to be highly regarded and respected. Another key characteristic that we will show later in David's life. When David heard about the blessings that had

---

[1] *Numbers 1:50-51*

fallen upon Obed-edom, he realized his anger against God was his own misguided, misunderstanding of God's commands and once he knew what was wrong, he retrieved the ark, handling it the right way, to bring it to Jerusalem. His second attempt was much better than his first, instructing the Levites to sanctify themselves and handle the ark. During the processional of the ark, [1]David dances and rejoices while sacrificing bulls and fatten calves along the way. His first wife Michal, watched from a window, mocking the behavior of her husband and said, "how distinguished the king of Israel looked today, shamelessly exposing himself to the servant girls like any vulgar person might do!" However, not fully understanding what happened and his reasoning for dancing this way, he declared, "I am willing to look even more foolish than this, even to be humiliated in my own eyes!" After securing the ark in the Tabernacle, David defeated and subdued the Philistines by conquering Gath, forces of Hadadezer son of Rehob, the

---

[1] *2 Samuel 6*

Arameans from Damascus, and secured chariots, gold, silver, bronze, and other gifts from the victories. He even showed kindness to Mephibosheth, Jonathan's son, and a descendant of Saul. However, David's next indictment of poor doyen leadership stems from Michal's disgust of David's dancing while ushering the ark into Jerusalem. 2 Samuel 6:23 offers several views of thinking concerning their relationship. The scripture says that out of all the wives of David, "to her dying day Michal, daughter of Saul, had no children." This notation suggests several things; David had no sex with her, he imprisoned her because of disloyalty, or banished her for speaking against the king (the previous two penalties are very likely since she was the daughter of Saul which she was referred as in verse 23, instead of his wife). The scripture is silent, and historians cannot draw a conclusion to her existence after verse 23 however, we can draw this conclusion, she was not present in 2 Samuel 9 because he inquiries about descendants of Saul's family remaining that he may show kindness too. Her absence yields a void and vulnerability in

David's life that causes him to impregnate Uriah's wife,

Bathsheba. This act of hedonism begins a series of bad

decisions and behavior stemming from pride and arrogance,

which could have easily come from the victory over the

Ammonites and his kindness toward [1]Mephibosheth, Saul's

grandson. Humanitarianism and pious rituals done with selfish

intent cannot earn your approval in the site of God. Paul

satisfies this query in 1 Corinthians 13:3, "if I gave everything

I have to the poor and even sacrificed my body that I could

boast about it, but didn't love others, I would have gained

nothing." After getting her pregnant, he would later have Uriah

killed because he refused to go home to his wife but instead

went back to his post at the door. An even worse display of

doyen leadership. After Bathsheba mourned the death of her

husband, David sent for her and made her his wife. All these

things were done to cover the immorality of David's decision

to sleep with her and God was very displeased. God sends

---

[1] *2 Samuel 9 KJV*

Nathan the prophet to tell David he was displeased and the penalty the ensued from his poor judgement. God reminds David how he anointed him king of Israel, saved him from the wrath of Saul, gave him his master's house, his wives, and the kingdoms of Israel and Judah and then told him I would have given you more. He also told him his family would live by the sword because he was immoral by taking Uriah's wife to be his own, causing his own household to rebel against him, turn his wives to other men in your site and allow it in public view. What he did it secret, God would make this happen openly in the sight Israel. However, the baby that was created would die. This one omission from his decisions was extremely necessary because only Bathsheba, Nathan, Uriah (who was murdered), and David knew about the child, if Israel knew what David did, rebellion would have broken out across the land against David and God. However, [1]David prayed that the baby would live, he fasted and prayed unto God laying on the floor hoping that God

---

[1] *2 Samuel 12:16 KJV*

would have mercy. Inevitably the baby died, and his elders were fearful of David's reaction if they told him, but he overheard them talking and realized what happened and displaying doyen characteristics, he got up from the floor, bathed, put on his clothes, and went to the Tabernacle. David's response to the child's death marveled his leadership. They could not understand his demeanor after days of fasting but clearly, he knew, and nothing could be done to change the baby's death. What a contrast from his humble beginnings. The least likely to be anointed by Samuel, hated because of your passion and desire to please God, and granted favor with so many to become king of Israel, only to lose Uzzah because you did not handle God's promises correctly, lose, banish, or imprison your first wife because she didn't understand your praise, impregnate another man's wife and have him killed, and lose the baby because God wouldn't let your bad decision live. However, one of the most quoted psalms was pinned by him, "have mercy on me, O God, because of your unfailing love and great compassion, blot out the stain of my sins. Wash me clean from my guilt and purify me from my sin. For I recognize my rebellion, it haunts me day and night. Because against you, and you alone, have I sinned." Through his bad decisions he learned the value of true repentance and contrition in the sight of God. But unfortunately, the [1]repercussions were imminent. The rape of Tamar by Amnon her brother, Absalom command to murder Amnon, Absalom flees and comes back home, only to steal the hearts of the people to rebel against David. Absalom would eventually be murdered by Joab and his armor bearers and David would be deeply sorrowful. David's obdurate behavior caused him great pain throughout his life and toward the end of his life, the anger of the Lord burned against Israel again because David took a census of the people for battle against the will of God. However, Joab did what David asked and after nine months and twenty days, he reported the number of people he counted. David again, realized he had sinned against God and another prophet, Gad,

---

[1] *2 Samuel 13-15*

told him God will give you three choices of punishments for your sins: three years of famine throughout your land, three months of fleeing from your enemies, or three days of severe plague throughout your land. He chose the plague and 70,000 people died from Dan to Beersheba. David built an altar unto the Lord and sacrificed burnt and peace offerings and the Lord answered his prayer for the land and stopped the plague on Israel. Once again, David does the right thing and God shows mercy upon him and the Israelites. His last act of doyen leadership was making Solomon his successor instead of [1]Adonijah, who was trying to make himself the king. This fulfilled the vow [2]David spoke to Bathsheba many years ago that her son would be king. What can be said about David's life? How do we draw a conclusion to his doyen leadership? Many years later Amos would speak an interesting prophecy that later Apostle James rehearsed the same prophecy, "afterward I will return and restore the fallen house of David. I

---

[1] *1 Kings 1:5-27 KJV*
[2] *1 Kings 1:17 KJV*

will rebuild its ruins and restore it, so the rest of humanity might seek the Lord including the Gentiles." Why not Moses Tabernacle? His son Solomon would build the temple but no references of this is spoken. Moses Tabernacle is the first and Solomon's Temple is the last, but why restore David's tabernacle? Of all the symbolic places where God dwelled with the people, David would be the only one who repented for his acts against God continually. No scripture is given for Moses smiting of the rock or Solomon taking the wives of other nations against the will and command of God. David's Tabernacle is a sign of repentance and contrition, the doyen leadership quality that transcends time and for generations, always attracted God's attention, provoking grace upon the people.

Chapter Nine

The Jesus Model

This model serves as the ultimate example of doyen leadership
and character. Though He was the Son of God, He indeed was
the Son of Man, living a life without sin and becoming
obedient to the cross (Philippians 2:8 KJV). This expository of
the canon will illustrate supreme doyen attributes throughout
his life and ministry. In the [1]apocryphal scriptures, Jesus' life is
chronicled to show the spiritual and supernatural giftings upon
His early life. However, the book's style and organization are
weak, with many major flaws as well as geographical and
historic errors. The Bible account of Jesus begins in the
Gospels of Matthew and Luke, outlining his birth to Joseph and
Mary. In the genealogy written in Matthew, Christ is shown to
be the legal king, in Luke His genealogy is shown as the Son of
Man, linked to humanity. [2]Luke's account takes Christ back to

---

[1] *Elmer L. Townes Theology for Today Copyright© 2002 by Wadsworth
Group, Chapter 2 – Bibliology, Section VI p.85-86)*
[2] *Luke 3:38 KJV*

Adam and Matthew's account proves that Joseph is the descendant of David through Solomon. Luke proves that the virgin Mary is likewise a descendant of David but through Nathan, not Solomon. Why is this so important? The King of the Jews must be born to a virgin woman who is the descendant of David however, a woman cannot be the recipient of the throne. Her conception by The Holy Ghost with heir to the throne, also needed a marriage to a man with succession and an unchallenged right to the throne. This birth was the legal access to be King of the Jews because of the descendancy to David through Joseph. At twelve years old, Mary and Joseph brought Jesus to the temple (primarily to fulfill the requirements of the Jewish custom of confirmation). [1]This confirmation, which is still in existence today, consists of preparing the candidate to recite passages of the law to rulers and doctors, which in conversation with him, test his knowledge, ask questions, and in return, he may ask questions that may come up from his

---

[1] *Becoming a Jewish Parent: How to Explore Spirituality and Tradition with Your Children by Rabbi Daniel Gordis. Harmony; 1st edition (October 5, 1999) ISBN-13 978-0609604083*

training. Jesus' parents were headed back home after the feast, when they discovered that Jesus had stayed behind at the temple, sitting with the religious teachers, listening, and asking questions eruditely. When they found him, [1]Mary said, "why did you stay here? We were frantic, looking for you." At that moment, the first sign of doyen characteristics surfaced. He told her, "Didn't you know that I must be in my Father's house?" It was very clear at twelve years old, His mind and motive were to fulfill God's purpose for Him in the earth, no matter who was in His life. Mary and Joseph did not understand what Jesus meant but He traveled back to Nazareth and continued his adolescent years with them. This could raise a question of disobedience to His parents which would be considered sin. However, His ultimate obedience to God the Father overrides anything the earth would require Him to follow. Jesus is God's Son, and his necessity to honor His true Father was supremely important and a test in his early years of ministry. The Bible does not speak much about Jesus'

---

[1] *Luke 2:45-50 KJV*

childhood, but we clearly recognize His oneness to God would preeminently dominate everything He did in the earth. With little information at twelve years old, the scriptures completely go silent, leaving scholars to speculate about his life. Some say He continued growing and learning in Galilee, being taught from His earthly father, carpentry, since Joseph was a carpenter (Mark 6:3 KJV). However, the one conclusion we can draw from this era is the complete silence and untraceable steps of His life, leaving many to wonder, why? If you are the standard that we are to follow, why would you leave eighteen years of your life unaccounted for? Maybe these "Silent Years" are another doyen teaching lesson. Much of these years speak to the personal life of Jesus Christ with a few displays of gifting and wisdom at twelve years old. Since Jesus consistently spoke of the Kingdom of God and the Kingdom of Heaven throughout his adult life, maybe these early years are a lesson to those who are gleaning from His life. All His life and events are not necessary for you to know to be a doyen leader, as well as those who follow in "your footsteps" to glean from your life.

To be very candor, too many people want information about your life to degrade and devalue you, rather than learn and grow from your life and experience. Silence sometimes has the loudest voice in teaching and development. The next time He is mentioned was Luke 3:23, indicating He was thirty years old, substantiating the eighteen years of silence concerning His life, and the first thing we see demonstrated was His obedience in baptism. Some would think if He were the Son of God, what is the need for baptism if you are already one with God? The scriptural answer is "to fulfill all righteousness." According to the [1]law of Moses, righteousness was required and according to [2]Levitical Law, at the age of thirty he had to be consecrated, which involved washing and anointing (Exodus 29:4-7). Another pertinent doyen characteristic is displayed through His baptism. Although He was the supreme authority, He was not above authority and submitted to the Messianic prophecy and priestly laws written before his earthly ministry. No leader can

---

[1] *Matthew 3:15 KJV*
[2] *Numbers 4:3 KJV*

declare or demand respect or prominence without demonstrating subordination and accountability to what is legally and ethically right. Baptism was not about sin, rather the door to God's mind (Kingdom of God) being open so you could walk into and understand His system (Kingdom of Heaven). To suggest baptism is the removal of sin suggest two incorrect theological truths: the first is Jesus Christ knew no sin (2 Corinthians 5:21) and the second was his conversation with Nicodemus never indicated the removal of sin but the ability to see the Kingdom of God (God's mind) and enter the Kingdom of Heaven (God's system) by being born again. The redemption from sin gave the Anthropos freedom from eternal damnation and access into heaven after death. Being "born again" regenerated the heart and mind so we could live with God's mind, in His system, on the earth. After His baptism, He returned from the Jordan River to be led by the Holy Ghost into the wilderness, where He fasted forty days and being tempted by the devil. During this extreme test of His doyen characteristics, the devil made every attempt to get Jesus to

[1]abnegate his authority. Christ did not go to the wilderness on His own; He was moved by God to face satan. This interaction would be the first time since Adam and Eve that the Anthropos would encounter the devil on the merit of earthly authority. A very important point should be observed about this encounter, this happened after Jesus was baptized, again proving His understanding and purpose to follow what was written. Adam & Eve were created and evolved by God, having direct access to His mind and system. Jesus being baptized as the Son of Man, gave Him access to God's mind and system, which now needed to be tested (forty is biblical testing or trial) by confronting the spirit that caused the fall of the Anthropos, the devil. This forty is seen throughout canonicity; in [2]Noah's day it rained forty days and forty nights, during [3]Moses' time, he thought Israel could be saved his way, only to flee and live in Midian for forty years, then returning to deliver Israel God's

---

[1] *Abnegate (as defined by Merriam-Webster.com) deny, renounce.*
[2] *Genesis 6:9-28 KJV*
[3] *Exodus 2:11-25 KJV*

way, and after rejecting the idea of the Promised Land, [1]Israel wandered in the wilderness forty years, until all those who did not believe died, then Israel entered the Promised Land. After the crucifixion of Jesus, He was resurrected from the dead and stayed in the earth an additional forty days before He ascended to heaven to be with God. During the temptation of the devil in the wilderness, there were a series of tests given to get Jesus to renounce His authority. The first was turning stones into bread, a replica of the devil telling Eve you can eat from a forbidden tree. Jesus was fasting during this test and creating bread would be an act of selfishness to satisfy His own hunger. Eve eating from the tree satisfied her own desire for knowledge, not the desire and command of God. The second temptation again focused on selfishness but this time around pride. By quoting Psalm 91:11–12, he wanted Jesus to pridefully use His authority to prove He had power to save Himself. He would later be tested again with this same theory on the cross

---

[1] *Numbers 14:33–34 KJV*

(Matthew 27:38-44). In both examples, the demonstration of power was to "save yourself" or "God saving Him." A doyen leader should never use power for selfish gain or demonstration but use the power of influence to promote the good of others, never oneself. Not only did he test His pride, but he picked an interesting place for the test, the highest point of the temple. The height of the temple is anywhere from 150ft upward to 200ft in the air. To throw yourself from such a place with angels catching you (which would be an act of suicide) would be quite a spectacle and unfortunately open a door of selfish acts in the life of the Anthropos, suggesting any act of suicide would be permissible for God to save you. This exegetical point coincides with Jesus' response, "don't tempt the Lord your God," which also suggests, even though I belong to God, it does not give me the right to tempt His protection, grace, and love. Taking Him to the top of the temple philosophically suggests as a leader (doyen) of the church, you can cast yourself into any act of selfishness or immorality and God will save you. Chapter III of Theology for Today offers a great observation that substantiates this point beautifully, "[1]no culture has ever risen above its religion and no religion is greater than its view of God. The most revealing insight about a man is his idea about God." To view God as a "safety net for anything I do immorally" would suggest an abuse of relationship and the misappropriation of His commands vs. His love. With two failed attempts to get Jesus to relinquish His authority, he puts all his cards on the table. He took Jesus into a high mountain where all the kingdoms of the world could be seen and told him, "I will give it all to you, if you will kneel down and worship me." This test would reveal several things and with this attempt to gain power, he unlocks a mystery to the Anthropos, and loses authority. The display of "kingdoms" illustrates territories in the earth that have a ruler; no kingdom can exist without a king. He reveals his ruling over these kingdoms and the key to dismantling his authority over them when he says, "I'll give them to you, if you kneel and worship

---

[1] *Elmer L. Townes Theology for Today Copyright© 2002 by Wadsworth Group, Chapter 3 – The Doctrine of God, Section I p.95-96)*

me." The exegetical proof of this fact is offered in [1]Jesus'

reply, "Get out of here, for the Scriptures says, you must

worship the Lord your God and serve only Him." Jesus never

said he did not have the authority of the kingdoms, He

established superior authority by submitting to the highest

authority, God, who established the world and all the

kingdoms. By not kneeling and acknowledging God and His

servanthood to Him only, broke the devil's influential power

over the Anthropos and realigned the earthly authority of the

kingdoms back to God. This temptation is defined in [2]Theology

for Today under Christology, The Temptation of Christ. It

states, not only was Christ equipped with a disposition to do

good (due to the presence of deity and the ramifications of the

hypostatic union), but He also was strengthened by the Spirit

(Luke 4:24, Acts 10:38), and when these two elements are

welded together with the immutable aspects of deity, they

make it impossible for Christ to desire evil or to commit sin.

---

[1] *Luke 4:8-11 NLT*
[2] *Elmer L. Townes Theology for Today Copyright© 2002 by Wadsworth Group, Chapter 4 – Christology, Section X*

Once this temptation was complete, he began to select the disciples, which would be the leaders of the Acts Church. Before choosing leaders, He was first tested in His character morally, ethically, and spiritually. This is the basis for doyen leadership and should never be circumvented to establishing leaders. These new leaders He chose would be the students of His life and ministry, to establish the New Testament church. However, in His choosing, there was a distinct relational variance He had with them. Throughout His ministry, we carefully witness His interaction with Peter, James, and John more than the others. In Matthew 20:20-28, the mother of the sons of Zebedee came to Him with James and John and knelt before Him asking for a favor. She said, declare my sons will sit on your right hand and the other on your left, when you come into your kingdom. This inquiry by their mother came because of the special relationship Jesus had with her sons. Although her request was callow (such appointment could only come through serving, not by special request or favors), she did recognize a special relationship between Jesus and her sons.

Later, Jesus heals the mother-in-law of Peter in Luke 4:38, while at the Lake of Gennesaret, He enters [1]Peter's boat and taught the people and when Peter could not catch any fish, He gave the command to let down his net to catch an abundance and it happened. James and John were partners with Peter and when they caught all those fish, the scripture says they forsook all and followed Jesus. An amazing display of doyen leadership, if I have influence in your life, I will prove it and cause you to follow me. There would be a series of events to follow, all moments of teaching and miracles with the twelve disciples however these three men seem to have favor with Jesus, which promoted more interaction and private moments of instruction and exposure. But in Luke 10, an unusual account happens. Jesus appoints seventy (seventy-two in certain translations) and sends them two by two into every city that He planned to visit. This is the only time this group is mentioned and adds an even stranger view of leadership by Jesus. And while you peruse the seventy he chose and sent out,

---

[1] *Luke 5:1-11 KJV*

and the theory of the twelve (of which three of them He

seemed to have a special relationship with), one of the three He

allowed to lay His head upon Him frequently, which makes his

leading tactics even more unusual to follow. This leadership

model would be viewed as the seventy-twelve-three-one

system of leading. It seems odd but let us take a very careful

look at this methodology. [1]Hermeneutically we could suggest

the seventy represented the seventy nations of Genesis 10

(descendants of Noah), seventy descendants of Israel that went

down into Egypt with Jacob (Genesis 46:27), the seventy elders

assembled by Moses (Numbers 11:16-30), and the seventy

elders of Israel who visit God with Moses. The biblical number

twelve represents divine government (Israel tribes which are

the Old Testament and the Apostles which represent the New

Testament), three represents the Godhead (trinity), and one

represents unification. This would suggest his appointments

---

[1] *Hermeneutics - Elmer L. Townes Theology for Today*
Copyright© 2002 by Wadsworth Group, Chapter 2, Section IX
p.88

and choosing were all very divine and purposeful to doyen leadership. It also shows another characteristic of leading, the multitude (seventy) that you can instruct without "babying," instruct them and let them go, the twelve that will establish order and structure, of which three you will have a close relationship with but one ([1]John) will have intimate proximity and access that will be with you when everyone else is gone.

Jesus had special moments of teaching and revelation to His leadership and purpose. In Mark 3:31, Jesus was speaking, and the multitude said, "your mother and brothers are looking for you." His response was very candor but important to His mission and leadership. He replied, "who is my mother and brother" not to insinuate no relationship with them, but to clarify anyone that will walk with Him shall do the will of God to be considered a part of His life. We know who Jesus' mother is, we know He had several brothers: James, Joseph, Simon, and Judas (Jude). Mary, James, and Judas became followers of Christ. Jesus says following Him will divide families in Mark

---

[1] *John 19:25-27 KJV*

13:12–13 stating, "and brother will deliver brother over to death, and the father over his child, and children will rise against parents and have them put to death. And you will be hated by all for my name's sake." In Matthew 10:35–36 Jesus makes a very strong statement saying, "I have come to set a man against his father, and a daughter against her mother, and a daughter-in-law against her mother-in-law. And a person's enemies will be those of his own household." But when it was tough to comprehend his conviction, He then said, "whoever loves father or mother more than Me is not worthy of Me, and whoever loves son or daughter more than Me is not worthy of Me (Matthew 10:37)." This seems very critical to have no apathy for your family. However, in many cases, your decision to be Christian is challenged by your family and Jesus sincerely understands (Hebrews 4:15). He instructs us how we should honor our parents (Matthew 19:19; Mark 7:9–13) but, He had to choose God regardless of His family's wants and desires. This is a doyen example of leadership, even if it requires leaving family, but He promises a greater reward will be given

(Mark 3:34–35; 10:29–30). When Jesus talks about His death

(Matthew 16:21-28), Peter rebuked Him suggesting He would

never suffer terrible things at the hands of the elders, the

leading priests, and the teachers of religious law. [1]But Jesus

spoke very sternly and said, "get away from me, Satan! You

are trying to trap me. You are seeing things merely from a

human point of view, not from God's will. If any of you wants

to be my follower, you must give up your own way, take up

your cross, and follow Me," indicating the same way He

surrendered and followed the will of God, so will they. This

response made a clear separation that even those who are

following Me, will only be able to follow through total

submission. This [2]proselytize of "family over everything" to

the regeneration of the heart through [3]soteriology is the only

way of walking admirably in Christ.

---

[1] *Matthew 16:23-24 NLT*
[2] *Proselytize (as defined by Merriam-Webster.com) to induce
someone to convert to one's faith.*
[3]*Elmer L. Townes Theology for Today Copyright© 2002 by
Wadsworth Group, Chapter 4 – Soteriology, Section II p.420*

The events leading up to His crucifixion were candid, showing vulnerability of His doyen character. While in [1]Bethany, at the house of Simon the leper, a meal had been prepared for them to eat. Mary, the sister of Martha and Lazarus whom Jesus raised from the dead were there. She was a devoted disciple who ignored the rumors concerning her commitment to Jesus. She sat at the feet of Jesus (Lk 10:39) even though that was not the place for a woman and at some point, Mary poured a pint of very expensive perfume on Jesus and wiped His feet with her hair. This was very unusual given Jewish women did not allow their hair to fall in public. This is an expression of deep devotion and could easily come across erotic, as it is viewed in most cultures. We do not know why she did it but obviously she was grateful for what Jesus did for her brother and her insight of Jesus' identity, power, and doyen authority. This act of wiping His feet, although seeming suspicious, would yield to absolute humility by her and substantiated shortly after when

---

[1] *Matthew 26:6-13*

Jesus washed the feet of the disciples. Despite criticism from Judas concerning the value, a year's wages at "three hundred denarii," Mary did not say anything. She let Him defend her by saying, "she has kept this perfume for my burial and has done a beautiful act of service for Me." Again, this unselfish act shows a few things concerning her: one, she seemed to know Jesus' death was preeminent, something that had escaped the disciples despite Jesus' constant reminders. Secondly, Mary had great sincerity for Jesus and was not moved to defend herself in the face of the people. This commitment to follow, as aforementioned earlier, proves that following Him and making Him our priority, will yield a deep understanding and passion for Christ, and give us great access and defense from critics who do not understand the value of a servant. After this meal, shortly afterwards the Passover would take place. Whether the Passover was a symbol of the Lord's Supper or not, there are commonalities between the two. The Passover looked back to the deliverance from the death angel in Egypt, after the blood had been sprinkled over the door posts prior to their exodus.

The Lord's Supper resembles Christ's death and the

deliverance from our sins. This "communion" reminds us of

His life and eschatology of His return. Three elements were

used in the Passover (Exodus 12:5-8) roast lamb symbolic of

Christ as mature meat necessary for mature Christians

(Hebrews 5:12-14), unleavened bread symbolizing the

separation of evil, and bitter herbs symbolizing the bitter agony

of death. The two elements in the Lord's Supper (Matthew

26:26-28) is the bread, symbolizing Christ as the "bread of

life" and food for our souls and the cup (the fruit of the vine),

symbolizing the work of Christ through the shedding of His

blood for the remission of our sins. In a moment of

transparency, He openly declares, "one of you will betray me."

This [1]eschatological statement would start the final moments

leading to His death. Everything He did to display doyen

leadership was clearly defined. He took on the likeness of men

---

[1] *Elmer L. Townes Theology for Today Copyright© 2002 by Wadsworth Group, Chapter 4 – Eschatology Chapter XIII p.713*

[1](Philippians 2:7), that I might be conformed to the likeness of Him [2](Romans 8:29), became poor that I might become rich in Him (2 Corinthians 8:9), He was willing to be hungry (Matthew 4:2) so I could be satisfied (John 6:35), He was thirsty in His suffering (John 19:28) so I would never be thirsty (John 4:14), became weary (John 4:6) that I might have rest (Matthew 11:28), was tempted (Matthew 4:1) that I might be delivered in the hour of temptation (Hebrews 4:15), became a servant (Philippians 2:7) that I might become a son of God (John 1:12), cried (John 11:35) that God might wipe away all my tears (Revelation 21:4), was troubled (John 12:27) that I might have a peace the goes beyond my understanding (Philippians 4:7), suffered persecution (Luke 4:28-29) that I might be of good cheer (John 16:23), was exceedingly sorrowful (Matthew 26:38) that I might have joy (John 15:11), was falsely accused and misunderstood (Luke 23:13-14) that I might have in Him a friend who understands (Hebrews 4:15-

---

[1] *The Scofield Study Bible Edited by: Rev. C.I. Scofield, D.D. copyright 1909, 1917 by Oxford University Press*

16), despised (Isaiah 53:3) that I might be exalted (Revelation 3:21), an outcast (Matthew 8:20) that I might be welcomed (Revelation 22:17), homeless in His own country (Luke 4:24) that I might have a home in glory (John 14:2-3), lonely (John 6:66) that I might never be alone (Matthew 28:20), forsaken (Matthew26:56) that I might never be forsaken (Hebrews 13:5), separated from God (Matthew 27:46) so I could be eternally connected (Thessalonians 4:16-18), felt the anger of God (Isaiah 53:3-11) so I would experience His love (1 John 4:10), endured darkness (Matthew 27:45) that I might be called out of darkness into His marvelous light (John 12:46), stripped of His robe (Matthew 27:31-35) that I might wear the robe of righteousness (Philippians 3:9, Revelation 19:7-8), became a curse (Galatians 3:13) that I might be blessed with every spiritual blessing (Ephesians 1:3), died (Matthew 27:50) so I could have life eternal (John 3:16), and wore a crown of thorns (Luke 23:33) so I could receive a crown of glory (1 Peter 5:4). To be betrayed by someone you chose to know and walk with you takes a deference to God's will that could only be described as supernatural. To have [1]depravity for someone who loved you so greatly is a true mystery. Herod's corruption is understandable, the Pharisees bitterness makes sense, how angry Annas and Caiaphas is valid, the negligence of Pilate can be reasoned, but Judas's betrayal is truly a mystery to understand. The synoptics do not reveal much about him or the reasons for selling him out. Why did satan choose Judas and not one of the others? We certainly know Jesus was aware from the beginning who his betrayer was (John 6:70), that Judas was called the "son of perdition" (John 17:12), that Jesus said that it would have been better for him not to have been born (Mark 14:21), and that Judas' betrayal was in fulfillment of [2]prophecy (Psalm 41:9). But there are some hints in the canon that might shed some light to why Judas betrayed Jesus. One reason could be his disillusionment of Jesus' purpose. Judas had probably seen himself as one of the "inner men" in

---

[1] *Depravity (as defined by Merriam-Webster.com) the quality or state of being corrupt, evil, or perverted.*
[2] *Elmer L. Townes Theology for Today Copyright© 2002 by Wadsworth Group, Chapter 4 – Eschatology Chapter XIII p.714-715*

an earthly kingdom which he had supposed Jesus had come to establish. In this kingdom Judas would be the key figure, and his people would be delivered from the oppression of Rome. He had gone along with Jesus, hoping that He would revenge the enemy and retore Israel. As time passed, there was a realization that his hopes were false, that he had fallen in with a Messiah of another kind. When Jesus talked about death; there was unfriendly opposition from the Jews. He spent time with the people to find out their temperament and perhaps Judas heard a rumor about the decisions in the meeting of the elders and feared that the Sanhedrin would want more than one victim but would condemn all those who followed Christ. Overcome by the possibilities, Judas thought he could fend off the pending danger and save his life; doubt and fear became the [1]ignominious of his betrayal. Being hurt by another can lead to betrayal. Judas had come to this point. He had been stung by his hypocrisy when a woman poured ointment on Jesus' feet

---

[1] *Ignominious (as defined by Merriam-Webster.com) deserving or causing public disgrace or shame.*

(John 12:1-8). The rebuke for his hypocrisy must have exasperated him because had been reproved for these faults on other occasions. To the rancor of this moment was added with envy, which always rises in vulgarity of misguided souls and with all his misgivings, we find him ripe for betrayal. Coupled with disillusionment and fear, there was his love for money, which is the root of all evil (1 Timothy 6:10). He had been chosen to be the treasurer, the one who held "the bag" (John 13:29). It is difficult to understand why a treasurer might think this is his money, but then, many church treasurers do the same thing when it comes to spending it for the Lord's work. But money was Judas's drive and having it was pleasing and gave him power. Talking about the poor, did not mean he cared for the poor. He was envious and greedy; but stingy as many [1]misers are. The consecration this King of the Jews and the honor that followed for a woman leader, made him suffer inwardly. Judas is a victim to the curse of money. Among the

---

[1] *Misers (as defined by Merriam-Webster.com) a mean grasping person; especially one who is extremely stingy with money.*

things which men have manufactured, money is perhaps the one which defiles the most and damage of the souls of men is quite evident. Everyone wants money and because of this, many have stolen, envied, and loved it more than life itself. This is what he wanted and to betray Jesus for thirty pieces of silver, cost him his life.

This moment of [1]fatuous betrayal cannot be overshadowed by the [2]fastidious event that happens when Jesus takes Peter, James, and John into Gethsemane Garden. The propinquity of His relationship with them would now be tried with a simple request, pray for me. Jesus would go off a distance to discuss the gravity of His purpose and God's will. After a careful review of the canon, we can clearly see the coalition between the Last Passover with the disciples and His prayer in the garden. It is also noteworthy to point out Jesus' prophecy of Peter's denial comes after Judas's betrayal which

---

[1] *Fatuous (as defined by Merriam-Webster.com) complacently or inanely foolish: silly.*
[2] *Fastidious (as defined by Merriam-Webster.com) very attentive to and concerned about accuracy and detail.*

offers a dichotomy of Judas' betrayal versus Peter's denial. Denial is a truth unaccepted, but betrayal is a truth accepted and disloyal too. Also, is it coincidental that the fall of man happened in a garden while the deliberation of man's redemption happens in a garden? Two very important moments in the life of mankind, both consultations are exclusive in the presence of God, with one yielding a [1]pejorative response from God while the other yields a strong [2]predilection from God. In a moment of sorrow and feeling overwhelmed, He is [3]laconic but precise in His inquiry to God, "[4]My Father, if it is not possible for this cup to be taken away unless I drink it, may your will be done." Three specific inquiries with the same drive, is there another way for this to work, if not let your will be done. This level of transparency shows a side of Jesus that every doyen leader should learn from. Although I am called to

---

[1] *Pejorative (as defined by Merriam-Webster.com) expressing contempt or disapproval.*
[2] *Predilection (as defined by Merriam-Webster.com) a preference or special liking for something; a bias in favor of something.*
[3] *Laconic (as defined by Merriam-Webster.com) using very few words.*
[4] *Matthew 26:39 & 42 NIV*

my position, excellent in my administration, consistent in my leadership, collegiately qualified and astute to my craft, sensitive in my governing, and unbiased in the subjugation of those I oversee, it does not mean that I agree with God's decisions or enjoy the weight of my leading when I know the appreciation will be minimal and at times without merit. His inquiry was not an abnegation of His responsibility but a moment between the Son of Man and the Eternal God, to express the burden and pain He was feeling. This anguish He was feeling caused [1]Hematohidrosis, which proves a deep contrition and overwhelming emotional distress thinking about what was pending to come. No leader should ever experience emotional trauma at this level trying to fulfill your duties and responsibilities of leadership, but this was not an ordinary man, and neither was His Father. This compilation of emotions displayed in these inquiries would certainly warrant a response

---

[1] *Hematohidrosis (as defined by Merriam-Webster.com) a condition in which capillary blood vessels that feed the sweat glands rupture, causing them to exude blood, occurring under conditions of extreme physical or emotional stress.*

suitable to his pain, right? God did not address Jesus' bleeding sweat nor his three inquiries of His will for His son. It seems extraordinarily insensitive, and his lack of response would almost suggest being [1]imperturbable. However, let us examine this conversation more carefully. The intrigue of His prayers does not match the weight of the moment, or does it? In every inquiry, He never changes His request, "let this cup pass from me." In observing this prayer moment, it is hard to formulate in one's mind the eschatological, ecclesiological, anthropological, theological comprehension of this moment was all based upon "a cup?" However, the "cup's" symbolism is far greater than its grammatical presentation. Thanks to Luke's gospel, we are afforded a candid view of Jesus serving at Passover, (modernized understanding of communion). Luke 14-20 NIV says, and He took bread, gave thanks, and broke it, and gave it to them, saying, "This is my body given for you; do this in remembrance of me." In the same way, after the supper He

---

[1] *Imperturbable (as defined by Merriam-Webster.com) incapable of being upset or agitated; not easily excited; calm: imperturbable composure.*

took the cup, saying, "this cup is the new covenant in my blood, which is poured out for you." He broke the bread, blessed it, gave it to the disciples and said, "this is my body given for you, do this in remembrance of me." He took the cup and said, "this cup is the New Testament in my blood which is poured out for you." The bread is for you, but the cup is for me. The cup (symbolizing the blood) which represents life goes to God. Exodus 12:7-11 NLT solidifies this point; they are to take some of the blood and smear it on the sides and top of the doorframes of the houses where they eat the animal. That same night they must roast the meat over a fire and eat it along with bitter salad greens and bread made without yeast. Do not eat any of the meat raw or boiled in water. The whole animal—including the head, legs, and internal organs—must be roasted over a fire. Do not leave any of it until the next morning. Burn whatever is not eaten before morning. "These are your instructions for eating this meal: Be fully dressed, wear your sandals, and carry your walking stick in your hand. Eat the meal with urgency, for this is the Lord's Passover. Why did He instruct them to put the blood over the door but eat the body of the lamb? The blood is God's, but the body is for you. Jesus was asking God, is it possible to let my life pass or is this your will? He asked this question because the cup (life through the blood) belonged to God and only God could grant Him the pardon. The lack of response was God's ultimate response, letting Jesus know there was no other way for redemption to take place. Our remembrance of this cup reminds us, no other life was qualifying and acceptable for the redemption of mankind accept the sacrifice God sent as the propitiation between Himself and His creation. The disciples sleeping was not an indictment to the lack of sensitivity but the reality of God's relationship with His son that they could not understand. Jesus did tell them to pray so they would not enter into temptation, indicating a dispensation that would require the same inquiry unto God with a requirement to adhere to His will without following selfish motives. Even when God does not answer, your intuitive knowledge through the Holy Spirit must be keen enough to lead you, even when a voice (God) will not direct you. The Holy Spirit and God are one and He will not lead you astray. This point would prove to be pivotal when Jesus was on the cross crying out, [1]"Eli, Eli, lama sabachthani? that is to say, My God, My God, why hast thou forsaken me?" God did not forsake His son and neither did the Son accuse Him falsely. Jesus cried, my God my God, not my Father my Father. God forsook the body but accepted the blood and Jesus cried to the judge, not to His Father. The Father will never forsake you, but the Judge must be just. This entire commentary and narrative about Jesus' life undoubtedly is the substratum of doyen leadership in any generation or dispensation. We have a Priest who can understand and lead us without compromise or biased judgment. We relish the honor of being redeemed by a savior who loved us enough to live amongst us, but not act like us, to present us not looking like us, but looking like Him.

---

[1] *Matthew 27:46, KJV*

Chapter Ten

Final Conclusion

From the beginning, my goal was to define doyen to the reader and through the inspiration and inerrancy of Theology, objective and subjective views of the canon, careful expository and hermeneutical extraction of scripture, and the magnified look at many of the forefathers who have demonstrated doyen leadership, but at times fail in their presentation and obligation. There is much to consider watching the lives of God's chosen. The pressure to live and exhibit the highest standards of obedience while leading people will push your emotions and aptitude to critical places that reveal the immorality of mortal liabilities. In Romans 7:15-20, Apostle Paul turned up the microscope of his life and spoke for us all when he said, "I do not really understand myself, for I want to do what is right, but I do not do it. Instead, I do what I hate. But if I know that what I am doing is wrong, this shows that I agree that the law is good. So, I am not the one doing wrong; it is sin living in me that does it. And I know that nothing good lives in me, that is, in my sinful nature. I want to do what is right, but I cannot. I want to do what is good, but I do not. I do not want to do what is wrong, but I do it anyway. But if I do what I do not want to do, I am not really the one doing wrong; it is sin living in me that does it. This is the plight of every person inspiring to be doyen in their lives. Are we doing wrong because we want to, at times, no? Do I ambitiously want to do right, at times, yes? But I am confronted with this other side of my life constantly fighting me and pushing me to do what I know is wrong. How can I achieve doyen when the other side of me abhors everything that is good and right? The Jesus model gives us the answer. Each model exhibited at some point, tried to make it on their own merit. The success of their lives during certain moments can trick you into a false sense of independency, thinking your succeeding by intellect or gifting alone. However, abnegation is how we succeed and function at the highest state of doyen. To "deny oneself" is to resist the urge "drinking your own Kool-Aid," thinking I am completely able to do anything without yielding my members to God. Having success is a temporary life achievement but to be successful requires a diligent yielding to humility and observing your temperament to see if you are trending in the wrong direction of gratitude, taking grace for granted. Confidence and arrogance look very similar, but they smell totally different. To put the two in true context; one understands it can do things very well and thinks it does not need anyone, while the other thinks the same thing but recognizes it cannot do anything without the help of somebody. The smell of arrogance repels people and God, which is why the scriptures says in Proverbs 6:17, "there are six things God hates and seven are an abomination unto Him. A proud look and a lying tongue," were the first two things mentioned, why? They are both synonymous with each other because typically prideful people typically lie to maintain a certain look and image. It drives their relationships, conversations, and motives, unconsciously, and at times display narcissism. These individuals cannot hold on to relationships very long because they use control to navigate the emotions of other people to satisfy their egocentric motives. These characteristics are nefarious. However, confident people have just enough pride to exhibit doyen without belittling others to achieve success. They know success comes from leading with you not leading above you. Its strength comes to make everyone great, not just themselves, but for a unification that promotes koinonia and harmony, not dysfunction and contention. If you are succeeding in any area of life, marriage, business, ministry, school, etc. look at the doyen you exhibit. If you are obdurate, difficult, and quarrelsome, chances are you are very noxious, trying to push the blame of the failure upon everyone else around you. Doyen leaders are responsible, accountable, and integral, never obscure in their motives and presentation. Doyen leaders strive for what is right in the sight of God and mankind, carefully monitoring their behavior because they know an audience is watching them to glean wisdom and direction. Do they always do right, no. Do they make mistakes, of course. Can they be mistaken in their presentation, sure they can. Why and how? Perception is one's reality and sometimes a misguided perception will distort one's reality and leave negative views to a misappropriated observation. Can you control the mind of another person? Through manipulation, you can, but with presentation and exhibition, no. Doyen is the ambition to be respected and highly regarded through experience but sometimes it can be misinterpreted. There are so many views and opinions to prominence, and what is respected is social statuses, perceptional wealth, and expert conversationalist that can fool the world to believe you are doyen. The image of doyen leadership seems to be greater that actual doyen leadership with this in mind, we are more concerned about the look of prominence than the working of prominence. We do not investigate or employ the necessary patience to ensure what we say is respectable is in fact respectable or even honorable. This is partly due to our prideful desire to look better, act better, and sound better than those around us. The artificial perception of doyen can be quite damaging to the moral conscience of society. When we look to an individual that we believe exhibits doyen attributes, there is an expectation applied that society would hold you to without wavering, in part because of the presentation given by the individual. Civic leaders, religious leaders, political leaders, educational leaders, judicial leaders, sports leaders, etc. are held to an expected standard of doyen because of their presentation in the sight of people. When an indiscretion takes place, the request for forgiveness and contrition will determine how society will respond. If no apology is offered or humility displayed to counter the indiscretion, typically society, for a season, will be dogmatic and unrelenting in its bashing and scrutinizing of the individual. Some have said this is wrong in lieu of each person's imperfections. However, if you accept all the praise and accolades from the perception of doyen without reservation, you must equally accept the scrutiny of your indiscretion, that came with no apology. Every aspect of doyen, in every category of human character, exhibited in every position of authority or prominence in the eyes of the public, will be held to this standard. There is no "grey area" to this notion. Ascending to places of prominence should be handled with dignity and honor. One can never be too careful in the display of your life in any area. Now, we know that people will find reasons to criticize every good thing you do but those individuals typically have little success in their own lives, so they find every reason to be negative and degrading. That is not your fault and does not warrant your response. Some critical thinkers are not problem solvers, but troublemakers look for a way to devalue anyone that is prominent without their help, approval, or influence. To be doyen will also require a thick skin against thin minded people. Doyen minded people are driven at a different frequency, to produce a different sound, yielding a different result. They do not settle for the average or the normal but push themselves to a standard beyond the normal expectancy of people. Their critical thinking of themselves is the fuel that drives their engines to achieve. Their ambitions are cisterns that always need to be filled. Even when things are good, they can be great. When things are great, they strive for excellent, and the drive continues in every aspect of their lives. There is a moment of gratification and an immediate reigniting of their drive to do it again, but better. It is a lifestyle they cannot resist. They are made different, function different, think different, and live different and all of it comes with no apologies. However, when they miss the mark, you will know it. They hold themselves to a standard that does not settle for less. They understand the plight to live at such a place, so they typically do not allow other people's scrutiny to move them at all because its ordinarily lower than their own internal standard. Doyen people have a different "bounce in their step" and when everyone stops, they continue because there is something else driving them. Once they become motivated, you do not need to look over their shoulder to see if their working. There are working because the motivation is driving them. On the other hand, they can be slow to move if there is an obstacle they cannot figure out. Some are accused of being procrastinators but that is far from the truth. The analytical mind of a doyen leader must always have the reassurance of competency before moving into a task. This plays an important role in efficiency, dexterity, and fluency to performance and demonstration. If you ever wonder why it takes a while for certain people to start certain tasks, it is in part to a challenge they have come up against that has not been solved and requires more thought before performance. Once they start, they are fine but if they have an issue with the assignment, you may need to give them a minute. If you lack motivation, competency, skill, or need to recalibrate your thinking because you have become stale in your ambitions and outcomes, you need a reset. No one can operate at the highest level all the time. Sometimes you push yourself so hard, that you push yourself out of motivation. When you begin to accept anything, no longer possess the same critical thinking about your performance, drag or have no energy to get tasks done, it is time for a break. This doyen characteristic is called "the burnout." The high-octane engine that drives you faster, longer, bigger, and better now runs mediocre to low average, which affect your attitude toward yourself and others around you. Doyen leaders are not just self-driven but affect everything and everyone around them. Even if you are not the "top person" or the person in charge but you have a doyen character, you affect so many things around you and the moderate to low engagement you offer slows down the environment and affects the character of everyone you touch. That break-time will serve you well and all the people around you. Sometimes it is hard to break away because you are driven to make things right and keep things optimally running well but every engine needs a tune up. The difficulty with stopping is the self-evaluation or internal perception of failure or incompleteness. The drive you possess does not like to stop in between anything, it wants to complete everything it starts, even at the expense of overload. Again, you are self-driven and at times you do not know when to quit or take a break. It is very important to have checks and balances to help you manage this characteristic in your life. You only have one life and sometimes you drive as if you can live forever but we know that is not true. However, the push to prominence and influence is a constant internal struggle of importance. Understand prioritizing and the need to enjoy the fruit of your work. You are indeed a different type of machine, with a different type of shifter but driving yourself to burnout does not help you or the people around you. You are your own worst enemy, pushing yourself too hard, too long, and too often. The optimal goal is to produce your ambitions, manifest your dreams, and have an excellent presentation but live to enjoy it all. Taking a break or pressing the pause button does not reduce your success or suggest that you are a failure but what it does inevitably prove to you is you are human and being human is completely ok because that is what God made you. You do not have to judge yourself as a failure just because you take break. Enjoy life and everything in it. God has blessed your life with wonderful characteristics, gifts, and dreams, all of which He wants you to see and enjoy but if you push too hard, you will self-destruct and live the remainder of your life with the disappointment of unfinished dreams. You did not give yourself this drive, but you can drive yourself too hard. Doyen is a beautiful characteristic that can only come from the most excellent creator in the universe, that is God, and He would never give you something so beautiful and so excellent, for you to burn yourself out before you can fully see all its benefits and blessings. You are uniquely designed to help so many nationalities and ethnicities, in so many situations across so many generations, it is unbelievable at times. Your ability to answer so many problems and produce so many solutions is the divine credibility of God, backing your doyen abilities. Everything you can see and everywhere you can go, is designed to receive the doyen in you. You are a masterpiece of wonderous gifting and your design to do it at the highest level of its presentation and demonstration comes from God. You cannot accept less than God's best for your life and those all around you see the good and the optimism that only God could have given. To know how empty you were, but now you see how full you have become is the testament of God's infinite doyen character, playing out in your life. He has pulled the scales from your life to allow a fresh new you to come out, showing the world how excellent He is in you. The changes you have already made, the lives you have already touched, are just the beginning to the splendor of God's wonderous love toward you and every time you see yourself in the mirror, you smile with a joy of knowing, the greatest demonstration of doyen was God's hands crafting a life that you did not know could operate at this level, see beyond the negativity of an environment starved and deprived of doyen leadership, use your life to reach into the negative and create the positive that others may feel the same joy you feel. You are a doyen leader, birthed at a time when we need you the most, cut from a fabric that only God could create, tested behind the scenes so no one could challenge it, oiled with His own hands to ensure longevity and elasticity, and motivated by the only one that could understand you, even when you did not understand yourself, this is who you are, what you are, and how you function.

This is the Making of a Doyen Leader.

About the Author

Bishop Tyrone Smith, D.TH is the Pastor & Founder of The Love Center in Baltimore, MD. He was born and raised in Owings Mills, MD and has served actively in church for over 30 years, faithfully in ministry for over 28 years, with 22 of those years as a pastor in the Maryland region. He was educated through the Baltimore Public School System where he graduated and later obtained his bachelor's degree in Theology. He completed his academic studies and holds a Master of Ministry in Leadership and satisfied all his academic requirements and graduated with his Doctoral Degree in Theology July 24, 2021. Consecrated to the sacred office of Bishop in the LORD'S Church in 2012, he serves as the Presiding Bishop of Prophetic Grace Episcopal Ecclesia, an organization he birthed with a specific desire to nurture and foster churches & leaders throughout the country.

He has a great respect for leadership and those he has served throughout the years. He attributes his early years of ministry to his first father in the faith, Dr. Herman Mack of Praise Temple Worship Center. As time has progressed, GOD sent him a man to nurture and father his life & destiny and honors him as his father in the faith now, Bishop Joseph A. McCargo Sr. Senior Pastor of the City of Hope International Worship Centre.

An entrepreneur with an exceptional grace for the 21st century marketplace, Bishop Smith is a Financial Advisor & Credit Specialist with an Insurance Producer License in Maryland, Washington D.C., Pennsylvania, South Carolina and Delaware. He's preparing to launch a Farmers Insurance Agency to provide auto, home, RV, and motorcycle insurance to combine his Life Insurance & Credit Agency into one office to provide financial & insurance services. He also owns & operates PGEE Graphic Design, a graphic and web designing company he founded in 2008 to provide an array of graphic, web, and media services across the country. He has served on the Board of Directors for Sanford Brown College as well as an Adjunct Professor for SBC, the Vice-President for the Baltimore Adolescent Treatment Guidance Organization a Treatment Foster Care/Child Placement Agency providing a full range of therapeutic and career development services to the youth (aged 10 and up) admitted into the program. However, the greatest accomplishment Bishop Smith relishes the most is his ardent love toward his wife and children. He is very happily married to Savonna Gooden-Smith, whom he married in November 2004, and they share in sincere & loving responsibility for their 3 sons: Dominic Jeriah, Jalen Takel, and Desten Tyvonne Smith. He is a humble but extremely confident man with a genuine vision for kingdom development.